Optimal Living 360

Praise for *Optimal Living 360*

"A revolutionary inspirational book . . . compelling and powerful." —*Readers' Favorite,* ★ ★ ★ ★ ★

"*Optimal Living 360* offers an extensive and encouraging action plan that puts you in charge of balancing life and prospering." —*IndieReader,* ★ ★ ★ ★ ★

"With humor and humility, Jain blends common sense with valuable research in this all-encompassing guide to life."

—*ForeWord* Clarion Review, ★ ★ ★ ★

"Balance, harmony, and an excellent return on your investment—in *Optimal Living 360,* Dr. Sanjay Jain offers the perfect trifecta on personal net worth. A must-read!"

—Kimberly Foss, CFP, CPWA,
New York Times bestselling author, *Wealthy by Design*

"*Optimal Living 360* is set to become the go-to handbook for finding fulfillment in your life."

—Cynthia Montgomery,
Harvard Business School professor, author, *The Strategist*

"Tired of digging through endless aisles of self-help books? Look no further than *Optimal Living 360*. Filled with extensive research as well as helpful personal stories, this book is the only resource you'll ever need."

—Stephen Viscusi,
CEO of The Viscusi Group, author, *Bulletproof Your Job*

"Practical and easy-to-read, Dr. Sanjay Jain's comprehensive guide for living answers every question you might have on how to make better decisions for a better life."

—Frances Cole Jones, president of Cole Media Management,
author, *How to Wow* and *The Wow Factor*

"No doubt about it, *Optimal Living 360* will give readers a great return on their investment."

—Dr. Michael Dow, author, psychotherapist and
addiction recovery expert, host of TLC's *Freaky Eaters*

Optimal Living 360

SMART DECISION MAKING
FOR A BALANCED LIFE

SANJAY JAIN, MD, MBA

GREENLEAF
BOOK GROUP PRESS

Published by Greenleaf Book Group Press
Austin, Texas
www.gbgpress.com

Distributed by Greenleaf Book Group LLC

For ordering information or special discounts for bulk purchases, please contact Greenleaf Book Group LLC at PO Box 91869, Austin, TX 78709, 512.891.6100.

Design and composition by Greenleaf Book Group LLC
Cover design by Greenleaf Book Group LLC

Cover images:
©iStockphoto.com/Alex Belomlinsky-bubaone
©iStockphoto.com/browndogstudios
©iStockphoto.com/appleuzr
©iStockphoto.com/Rouzes
©iStockphoto.com/tuncaycetin
©iStockphoto.com/ragandi
©iStockphoto.com/lushik

Cataloging-in-Publication data
Jain, Sanjay (Sanjay Kumar), 1970-
     Optimal living 360 : smart decision making for a balanced life / Sanjay Jain.—1st ed.
     p. ; cm.
     Issued also as an ebook.
     ISBN: 978-1-60832-583-2
     1. Decision making. 2. Well-being. 3. Self-management (Psychology) 4. Life skills. 5. Quality of life. 6. Life change events—Psychological aspects. I. Title.
BF637.D43 J35 2013
158   2013934051

Part of the Tree Neutral® program, which offsets the number of trees consumed in the production and printing of this book by taking proactive steps, such as planting trees in direct proportion to the number of trees used: www.treeneutral.com

TreeNeutral®

Printed in the United States of America on acid-free paper

14 15 16 17 18   10 9 8 7 6 5 4 3 2

First Edition

This book is dedicated to my family, including my wife, Priti, and my two sons, Milan and Arjun. I also want to dedicate this book to those who have left this world too soon, including my unborn twins; my uncle, Dr. Rajiv Dhabuwala; and one of my close childhood friends, Keith Huber, who died in his thirties from kidney cancer.

CONTENTS

Preface

Warning! I want to give you a heads-up first before you read any further. This book may actually give out too much information. Yes, that's right: TMI. Conventional wisdom and rule of thumb suggest sticking to only a few topics. Guess what? This is not your conventional book. I am not going to follow the herd on this one.

Why not? Because we all live multidimensional lives as human beings we have a complex makeup in a very complex world. We can't afford to be masters of one domain yet be completely deficient or devoid in all the others. No one is perfect, including yours truly. We all have our unique strengths and weaknesses. I have had my share of life's blunders, tragedies, failures, or whatever you want to call them. Yes, I have fallen on the mat quite a few times. Despite being battered and bruised in the figurative sense, I have continued to pick myself up.

My journey of ups and downs has given me a greater appreciation of life's many twists and turns. I have had to learn about some of my own imperfections and insecurities. How does one deal with and reconcile them? The fact is they simply aren't limited to one particular category. In terms of spirituality and religion, I have had times when I had internal conflicts and doubt to a point of existential confusion. In terms of health, I have had a few scares along the way. My relationships have come with their challenges as well as their rewards. And, of course, I have not been immune to the recent economic storm.

How do you navigate and survive this wilderness called life? There is so much information out there; it's a bit overwhelming to try to gain perspective and understanding. It's even more frustrating when you try focusing on one problem but still need help with several other issues. Who can you go to for help? What should you read? When I was in that situation, I didn't want to walk out of a bookstore or library with ten books on various self-improvement subjects. I wanted to find one book that would give me a snapshot of life. I never found it—until now. It's right here in your hands. You are holding it.

This book was born from my own search for clarity and meaning. My goal is for you to get the absolute maximum of information possible from it. In other words, I want you to have a very high return on investment (ROI). Toward that end, I've included everything but the kitchen sink in this book. I want every page you turn to be of great value.

Keep in mind that you don't need to be a superstar in everything. If you are simply well informed, you will be able to reach levels of mastery in several areas. Why not? We should all strive to find balance in life and excel in as many areas as we possibly can. I have complete confidence you can do this. We all have potential; by tapping into it, our limits are boundless.

In reading this book, you have taken the first step toward better living. However, don't expect to make wholesale changes overnight. It's a process. Rome wasn't built in one day. This book is meant to kick-start your journey, to give you a few pointers to build on. You will likely have to go back and reread and review things on occasion. Once you start noticing positive results, I am sure you will want to keep going. Even if you're not ready for immediate change, simply being aware of the possibilities will help you set future goals.

So let's not delay! Let's get started on this journey together. Time is too precious to waste!

1

Optimal Living 360, the Basics

"Life's time is never found again."
—*Benjamin Franklin*

Time's a Wastin'!

We humans are an ambitious lot. We set out on our paths to start families and to forge careers. We create art and aspire to know the secrets of the universe. We work at our daily jobs to make a living. We exercise to perfect our bodies. We read all there is to know about our favorite subjects, and we practice to be the best we can be in our fields. Somewhere in the middle of our ambitions, we want recreation, and we have to make time for that, too.

Time is the greatest of life's gifts and the greatest of life's challenges.

It is the most valuable and limited resource we have. For many of us, there are so many enjoyable, challenging, and simply compelling things in the world that our choices can appear endless. The simple truth is our time here is limited. Your lifetime only comes around once. Best make sure you utilize it to its fullest potential.

CORE ASSETS IN LIFE: ASPIRES

As we journey through our given time on earth, it is important to develop an understanding of the major commonalities of our lives. No matter what words we use to describe ourselves, we all connect in some way with the same safety, physical, intellectual, relationship, economic, and spiritual aspects. I call them the Core Assets, and they are best remembered with the simple acronym ASPIRES:

Assets

Safety

Physical

Intellectual

Relationships

Economic

Spiritual

Let's look at each of these categories more closely.

SAFETY

Safety is an often overlooked and underrated aspect of the Core Assets. It deserves much more attention. Think about it: You could be doing everything right in life. You could have a great marriage, beautiful children, and a lucrative, rewarding job. Tragically, one split second of stupidity or simple bad luck can wipe it all away. Safety is therefore a state of awareness and prevention that binds the other aspects of our lives together in order for us to thrive fully.

PHYSICAL

Physical health and well-being involve a multitude of factors including genetic predispositions, biochemical disposition, and many other factors you can't control. However, it also includes factors you can control, such as exercise, nutrition, and your cholesterol, blood sugar, and blood pressure levels. We all want to feel well, and to do that we must decide how best to prioritize physical health in the middle of all the things we do and care about.

INTELLECTUAL

Fulfilling the mind falls in the domain of intellectual health. Education is a big part of that, and it can be broken down into three parts: basic academic learning; vocational learning, through which you can acquire the skills of a trade and valuable real-life experience; and continuing lifelong education. All of these forms of education ultimately help you build your career.

However, intellectual well-being does not rely only on education. Your overall mental state needs to be taken into account. Do you suffer from depression? Is your self-esteem intact? Are there any underlying psychiatric conditions? Do you have problems with concentration and focus?

Last is leisure—a completely valid aspect of intellectual health.

Sometimes a day on the golf course or at the beach is the best thing you can do for yourself to de-stress from all that's going on in your life.

RELATIONSHIPS

This category encompasses more than just your ability to maintain a relationship with a life partner. You have some sort of relationship with everyone of any significance in your life. Your connections with all your family members constitute relationships, as do your bonds with friends. You may have various relationships with workmates or fellow students. More broadly, you may have relationships within larger groups, from the crowd you hang with in your neighborhood to the culture in which you were raised, which can play a big part in your ethnic or gender identity.

Each type of relationship and each individual relationship will present its own set of potential joys and challenges. The health of your relationships may change depending on how you and the other parties involved work together on maintaining them.

ECONOMIC

Economic health, in the most basic terms, has to do with your cash flow. And that has a lot to do with the career you choose, which certainly matters a great deal in terms of how it provides for your needs. With our current economic situation, do you still have a job? If not, how are you managing?

The overall strength of your financial situation is based on all the factors that bring you money, and that is what's called your *economic health*. Each aspect affects every other, and what we spend most of our time doing will color the rest of our experiences. For example, some people choose careers that provide economic well-being but that may squash the joy out of everything else.

SPIRITUAL

Your spiritual health and well-being are most vibrant when your worldly outlook keeps you feeling positive and connected. They give you hope, guidance, and a sense of purpose in the grand scheme of things. They bring you comfort and understanding in hard times.

Spirituality comes in all shapes and sizes. One person may find solace in the stars, planets, and other great wonders of the natural universe, while another may find it in watching a dandelion tuft float by. Spirituality is a state of mind commonly confused with religion, although, you can certainly be spiritual without being religious. Religion has its place in that it provides a sense of identity around which you can structure your spirituality, but both religion and spirituality have their values.

LIFE CURRENCIES

It would be easy to list hundreds of examples of where each individual Core Asset comes into play. However, in life they never function individually. When you fall in love, at first it might feel like that relationship is the only thing that matters. If you stay in that mode for too long without regaining personal centeredness, your sense of spiritual balance may be compromised. And, depending on the person you fall in love with, you might want to watch the bottom line of your bank account.

Everything is interconnected. All the moving parts together form an intricate, complex machine. Unfortunately, this means when you give attention to one Core Asset, it inevitably uses time and resources that could go to another. Any frazzled parent trying to take care of the kids, work for a living, and be a loving partner has an intimate relationship with this dilemma. No matter what you choose to do, something else will inevitably be left undone. We compromise based on the choices we make, and that compromise is typically known as our *opportunity cost*.

In order to obtain what we want, we must expend some form of currency. Time is the primary currency we use to obtain the Core Assets. Others include energy currency (further broken down into physical, mental, and spiritual energy); social currency; and of course, our financial currency or money. The decisions we make about how to spend our currencies ultimately shape how we lead our lives—whether they're fulfilling or not. Thankfully we have the power to make decisions with the necessary moderation and balance to put our Core Assets to the best use.

RETURN ON INVESTMENT (ROI)

To the uninitiated, the language of the world of finance can sound very specialized. It isn't surprising that many people leave it up to others to worry about the finer points of capital gains and losses, write-offs, and portfolio theory. However, it still seems relevant to use some financial terms in this section. I hope you won't let it scare you.

A deep study in finance can eventually lead you to some pretty complicated formulas—such as return on investment, or ROI. You can use ROI to help you determine whether an investment will meet or has met expectations on its return. In its most simplistic form, you can think of it as your net gain divided by the cost:

$$\text{ROI} = \frac{\text{Gain from Investment} - \text{Cost of Investment}}{\text{Cost of Investment}}$$

Seeking a good return on investment—that is, getting a positive reward for what was invested—is a useful way to think about money and a great way to think about life. Your personal plan for aspects you want to emphasize and the kind of effort you want to put into them will help you maximize your ROI.

MAKING THE MOST OF LIFE

I am a regular guy who has tripped through life, making mistakes just like everyone else. Sometimes it takes road bumps to inspire us to share what we have learned along the way. During the trying times, we look for meaning, and eventually an "aha" moment occurs. This book offers some of my insights and what I have learned from those moments.

I am a doctor. I paid my dues by going through the rigors of school and training, and I have been in practice for many years. I enjoy what I do, especially the fact that nearly every day I am able to help save lives in some capacity.

However, I didn't always aim to be a doctor. Growing up in a modest Midwestern city in Ohio, my interests were broad—I enjoyed school subjects from science to the arts. Ultimately science won out, and I eventually took part in an accelerated MD program; I started college the day after my high school commencement. Despite the advantage of saving me a few years in school, there was definitely an opportunity cost in terms of not being able to participate in some of the more traditional college activities.

After medical school I did a medical internship in Detroit, not too far from the infamous 8 Mile Road. My first experience with death happened there: Caught in a sudden traffic jam, I realized there had been a terrible accident only a few cars ahead. I got out to see if anyone needed help, only to find scattered body parts and a dead man lying on the street. During my time as an intern, I also had the unfortunate experience of watching someone stricken with the AIDS virus die. The family members' anguish and tears of grief remain a disturbing memory.

My subsequent years in Los Angeles brought me close to another rough neighborhood—South Central. And once again I was exposed to disturbing scenes of people suffering from traumatic injuries such as gunshot wounds, stab wounds, and severe blunt injuries from fights or vehicle accidents. It was indeed a violent area.

During that time I became aware of the pain and fragility of life, and that has stayed with me in my professional life—and worked its way into my home. Watching my grandfather die slowly in a hospital brought back that feeling of sad inevitability. More shocking was my uncle's passing. He was a doctor in his early fifties who had never smoked a day in his life. Still died of lung cancer. Two of my friends also passed away, both in their late thirties—one from kidney cancer and the other from a sudden heart attack. My feelings of personal loss that resulted from these deaths drove home the point of making the best of the time we've got.

But we aren't here to dwell on death. This is about how to live life to the fullest. Mine is full of things I wish I'd known earlier and factors I could have taken into consideration. When we take the time to consider what has impacted our lives and the things we might like to change, it gives us insight into how to create a positive ROI for life.

LEARNING FROM EXPERIENCE

I used to be the king of quick decisions. This was never truer than when it came to making financial decisions. Initially I never had the skills or the patience to think them through. Surprise, surprise. Isn't that what doctors are known for—poor business sense?

Prior to earning my MBA, some of my investment choices really cost me. With health-care reimbursement in perpetual decline, I saw a need to look at alternative income—real estate, stocks, and options, just to name a few. Being ever the optimist, I never stopped to think about the possibility of losing on them. My real estate ventures in particular were poorly timed, given the subsequent crisis. I lost not only money but also my peace of mind. It almost led me to the brink of bankruptcy.

What did I learn? My life currency expenditures (time, money, energy, emotions, and social) far exceeded any gains I made. I tried to take a shortcut in life, to get more things more quickly, and I wound up losing more than I could have imagined. Had I been a patient turtle instead of a flippant hare, I may have been better off.

Clearly I have made my share of mistakes in life. I wish someone had been there to help me through them and to give me some clues about what might bring happiness and what might not. My parents did a great job, but being the first generation here in the United States from India, their knowledge of the intricacies of this new and different culture was limited. More guidance with an awareness of those facts could have led me through the twists and turns and helped me make better choices more easily and in less time.

NOW OR NEVER

Why not now? If not now, when? It's never too late to start a new habit or new life assessment. The current level of world anxiety points to the need for a shift. In the United States, many people and businesses are still reeling from the recent financial crisis. Many live in a heightened state of fear and mistrust. Some are just starting to pick themselves up and dust themselves off, and there is a sense of overarching anxiety that has gone global.

We are constantly bombarded, if not with financial worries then with the specter of terrorism or the information overload that many of us experience in our 24/7, love/hate relationship with the Internet. Most of us are not world leaders and only some are activists, so the majority of us need to find strategies to make a certain amount of peace with what goes on in the big world. In our daily lives, most of us have more control than we know. The sooner we realize this, the greater our potential for creating healthy living in all the aspects of our lives that matter most.

Information bombards us at various levels of urgency. Often one source of information doesn't take any others into account. A do-it-yourselfer might tell me I'd be better off remodeling my bathroom myself, but that person doesn't realize that the time I'd spend, the frustration I'd endure, and the money it would cost to have someone clean up the mess I made would hardly be worth it. A doctor might prescribe a medication without discussing alternatives—or the fact that without insurance it will cost fifty dollars for each pill. In even the simplest of lives there are decisions to make, and in our contemporary world, not many of us are monastic. Getting stuck in a constant inability to synthesize information or make good decisions leads not only to poor choices but also to poor health from the stress that is the likely result. The best time to start working to reverse that trend is now.

Time is something you can never get back. Good decision making and smart life planning are not just for older folks. I have a lot of vitality at my age, but there are a few things I wish I had done earlier that I can't do now. My shoulders and back hurt a little bit more at times, and healing can take a little longer. I notice myself crossing the invisible line from invincibility to vulnerability. So if you want to climb Mount Everest, you'd best make the decisions that will lead you there when you're younger and perhaps more physically capable. For young people and everyone else, there is no time like the present to maximize your ROI to make the most of your health and enjoy the years you have.

As someone who always appreciates other people's advice, I've found it frustrating that I had to go to so many different sources to get it. And afterward it took quite some time to synthesize it. I hope you can get the big picture—see the forest for the trees—through this book.

2

Core Assets for
Integrative Decision Making

YOUR PERSONAL LIFE
ASSET ALLOCATION

Financial advisers sometimes like to give people ballpark figures on where they ought to invest their funds during various life stages. This is known as *asset allocation*. The mantra usually is that if you're in your twenties, invest 70 percent in stocks because you're at a stage when you can take more risks. Once you're in your seventies, they say, play it safe with only 20 percent in stocks. This is the conventional wisdom when it comes to taking care of your money. Remember, though, when it comes to life we have a whole lot more going on.

Instead of thinking about the various places you could invest your money, such as stocks, bonds, or money market funds, imagine having a plan for your Core Asset allocation. In other words, how can you allocate your life currencies—time, money, emotions, social, and energy—in order to balance your Core Assets? Is the bulk of your currency going toward what's most important? And, for that matter, what is important? Life is always a work in progress, so anything you craft today on the topic might change tomorrow. That's perfectly okay. Just as any financial plan you developed at age twenty should change when you reach age thirty, forty, fifty, and beyond, the parts of life you need to emphasize now will shift as you grow. Anyone who thinks deeply about Integrative Decision Making is someone who ASPIRES.

WHAT IS INTEGRATIVE DECISION MAKING?

People have to make choices all the time. Some may be fairly simple while some may be quite complex. The consequences of our choices will lay the foundation for our overall well-being.

There are many ways people can make decisions, just as there are many different outcomes that may arise as a result of the pathway you choose. A CEO may use game theory in decision making, whereas an economist may use a rational form of thinking. Doctors may use an algorithmic method based on evidence and data. A detective may use deductive reasoning to reach a conclusion.

Other approaches include systematic, hierarchal, impulsive, decisive, flexible, and Integrative Decision Making. It would be beyond the scope of this book to go through each of these approaches; just know that each type has its own decision-making methodology. In the context of what we want to achieve, we will focus on Integrative

Decision Making. Why? Simply because it integrates all of the Core Assets in the ASPIRES model.

YOU'RE THE CEO—YOU DECIDE

At first it might sound a little daunting to get started with Integrative Decision Making. Even when making a relatively rash decision, you might get that frustrating feeling of weighing far too many options. A well-thought-out decision might feel like it has even more moving parts.

Not to worry. Taken into consideration one bit at a time, it's really not so bad. Determining your priorities and figuring out your best options are great uses of your time. That's how you maximize your chances of the best outcomes or maximum ROI. You know you want to go there. I can tell, because if you've read this far, you have high ASPIREationS.

One of the really helpful things about Integrative Decision Making is that it can be used for small or big problems. Learn this method of thinking, and you pretty much have it.

For every choice there are a few steps you'll want to take:

1. **Define the problem**. What is the goal or objective that needs to be achieved? In other words, what is the target or overall purpose?

2. **Frame the problem**. We will use the ASPIRES model as our frame. We will consider each of the Core Assets when making our choices.

3. **Develop all your options**. You do this by collecting facts, data, or whatever relevant information is available. Of course your sources need to be reliable and useful, not distracting or irrelevant.

4. **Analyze your options**. Ask yourself what the pros and cons of each option are and how it ranks in terms of your priorities. What are your chances for success or failure for each option? Also, each option should be evaluated as to whether it can be implemented realistically.

5. **Make the decision**. Do this through the process of elimination. It is much easier to eliminate options you don't want instead of those you do. With the options left, you may need to go back to step three and gather more information.

6. **Execute your decision**. Once it's made, commit to it and make it happen. Nothing is worse than going through a carefully thought-out process and not being able to execute it. Of course there may be some unknown obstacles along the way. However, anticipating as many potential obstacles as possible will leave you well prepared for contingencies.

7. **Debrief yourself**. This is time set aside for reflection on and learning from your choice and subsequent outcome. Did it meet your expectations? What could you have done differently? This is called *learning from ones life's experiences*. This is where wisdom is typically born. It is a crucial process in self-development no matter what the outcome is.

This whole process of Integrative Decision Making will bring you the greatest overall ROI. It factors in all aspects of your life that are important to you. While a professional adviser may be best equipped to tell you what he thinks about a certain situation, he will not understand the other aspects of your life that need to be factored in. In other words, you alone are empowered to execute your ROI.

Let's examine this method by looking at a relatively simple example.

WHAT IS THE BEST ROI FOR MY TRAVEL PLANS?

Say you need to make a decision about a vacation. Where will you travel to, and why? You could choose a destination just because it sounds like fun. But why not get even more out of the experience?

To maximize your ROI for this vacation, begin with the basic steps to Integrative Decision Making. In step 1, define the "problem." In this case, it is an opportunity to choose a vacation destination. In step 2, frame the problem using the ASPIRES model. Consider your Core Assets:

- **Safety:** First, anytime you travel, safety must come into play. Take the time to do a little research on where you're thinking of going. If you want to travel abroad, is the specific location reputed as safe enough by reliable sources? Having a strong sense of your personal risk tolerance plus a dose of good common sense will help you tremendously here. Read up. Make sure you're not headed for a war-ravaged city when you're hoping for uninterrupted tranquility.

- **Physical:** Would you like this trip to be rugged or invigorating? Would you prefer a relaxing trip with few physical challenges?

- **Intellectual:** Would you prefer going to lectures on your favorite academic subject or taking a writing course? That sort of thing might be perfect, or you might prefer to give your brain a rest with a strawberry daiquiri on a faraway beach.

- **Relationships:** How will your various relationships fit in with this trip? Thinking of a sexy getaway with your significant other? How about a fun family vacation with something of interest for people of varying ages? Will you want to rendezvous with friends or other associates somewhere along the way? Instead you might say "forget everybody" and make it a go-it-alone adventure.

- **Economic:** Of course you can't forget the economic part of the decision. Are you looking for a high-end, luxurious trip? Are you considering a low-cost outing that involves camping, low-budget motor lodges, or even couch surfing?

- **Spiritual:** What is the spiritual importance of this trip? Will you be probing your subtle consciousness or seeking out a religious awakening? If such a thing is a high priority in your life, you might be inclined toward something like a meditative retreat or a once-in-a-lifetime pilgrimage to a sacred site. Don't be too hasty, however.

In step 3, develop your options. Now that you've gotten a sense of the most important elements of this trip, let's look at some options. You decide you aren't getting any younger, and you don't want to miss out on perhaps a last shot at something adventurous. The three vacations you would like to consider are: an exotic trip to Africa for a safari; a trip to Katmandu, Nepal, to get close to Mount Everest; or a less exotic but still exciting trip to the Blue Ridge Mountains.

In step 4, analyze your options. Which has the best deal available during the time you want to go? What will the weather conditions be like? Who will be willing to join you? There is some civil unrest in the part of Africa you wanted to tour. This is a safety issue. The airfare to go to Nepal is high for the time of year you want to travel.

This is a financial issue. These are just a few points to analyze. Use the process of elimination.

In step 5, you make the decision. You settle on a trip to the Blue Ridge Mountains. You decide that getting some exercise and spending time with family are the most important things to do on this particular outing. You can take advantage of the great hiking trails all around the region, get some vigorous exercise, and catch up with people you haven't interacted with in years for more than a quick phone call. This means you'll be prioritizing the physical and relationships Core Assets.

Spirituality wasn't an important factor in the decision, so the fact that you find the mountains inspiring is a bonus. The bed and breakfast where you'll stay is a bit pricey, but the economic hit is okay to balance out private time and visiting time. You decide to read up a little on hiking safety and will abide by any recommendations from the rangers or posted signs at the trail sites. Other than that you decide that worrying too much about safety isn't practical in this case.

Intellectual health doesn't really figure into this trip; you've decided there will be other times and other trips to exercise the brain. From this trip you'll get everything you want most, and maybe there will be pleasant surprises along the way.

Step 6 is when you execute your decision. This can be the most difficult step—going out there and making it happen. For many people planning is easy, but the follow-through can leave a lot to be desired. You owe it to yourself to reap the rewards when you work so hard to create the best plan. So go call your relatives, book the room, and take the time off from work while you're thinking of it. Go for it!

Finally, in step 7, it is time to debrief yourself. You can do this on the long flight back home. Or perhaps you can debrief a few weeks later, when you gather with your friends and family again, sharing your stories of heroism and bravado. Yes, it was a great trip. It was a wonderful use of your life currencies. You have realized a very high ROI based on the amount of enjoyment and connection with those specific slices of the Core Asset pie you chose as most relevant this time around.

STUMBLING BLOCKS TO AVOID

Trying to make the right choice takes not only time and discipline but also an awareness of some potential roadblocks along the way. There is a human tendency to stick with the status quo or become entrenched in a comfort zone, which can make change a bit difficult. When making a decision to maximize your ROI, it's important to put yourself in the right frame of mind by eliminating distractions. Go to a quiet place and avoid the Internet, your smartphone, and anything else that might tempt you.

It's most important to avoid a defeatist mentality; you must have confidence that you will make the right choice. However, this has to be balanced by not being overly confident. Trust yourself and your instincts. If it gets to be a bit complex, quitting or procrastinating won't help. By breaking it down into pieces, you can easily make the right decision for yourself. Let's take a look at another example.

WHAT IS MY ROI ON BUYING VERSUS RENTING?

As you can see, if you really pay attention to details, there are quite a few decisions to be made beyond where to go on vacation. Don't worry—once you get the hang of thinking in terms of maximizing your ROI, you'll be making good decisions in record time.

What to do on a five- or ten-day trip isn't the most challenging decision you'll face. Now it's time to take a longer look at a more complex problem. This time let's think about what you need to decide when it's time to relocate. Where will you live? Once you have a bead on that, should you buy or rent?

If you ask around, the advice you'll hear from one helpful person is very likely to conflict with the next chestnut of wisdom. Once you get used to the decision-making process, you don't necessarily have to go through each step. It will become more natural and less mechanical. Let's take a look.

First things first: Where in the world would you like to go? First you can run through the Core Assets on your own, and figure out which would be most important in a move. A common response is "close to work or family." From an economic perspective, it is also well worth it to examine laws and ordinances in the places you consider. For example, if you're considering living near the border of Florida and Georgia or Florida and Alabama, with all other things being equal, which should you choose? When you look at the economic bottom line and establishing security, the answer is simple: Florida. Based on current law in that state, as long as you've lived in your home for at least forty months, your homestead has unlimited protection from creditors. Your IRA has the same 100 percent protection. To top it off, there is no state tax. This is a huge advantage. It really does pay to check out the possible legal and economic advantages of one state over another.

While you work on deciding whether renting or buying is the best option in the location you've selected, take a look at ASPIRES. What are the general qualities you need in and around your new digs? How will your heart and consciousness feel in any potential new dwelling? Your spiritual health in that place might depend on specific beliefs or sensibilities you hold. If you are most comfortable when your place is balanced by the Chinese practice of feng shui, having a home that gives you a clear square or rectangular shape to work with will be important. Some followers of Hinduism find it auspicious for the home to face east or southeast. If you're Amish, central heating is likely not welcome in your home. You will also want to have a place large enough to host church meetings. A tenet of Sharia Law is that paying interest is forbidden. In that case there may be limits on the cost of a home that would fit within those bounds. You may simply enjoy living near your favorite synagogue, congregation, sacred circle, or near like-minded individuals.

If you've already chosen the basic location for your next home, physical health probably played a big role. Living where it is warm is essential for good health for some. Maybe you've decided you're up for climbing the steep, hilly streets of San Francisco, or maybe the flat, wide streets of Indianapolis might be a better fit. Now do you want to take part in sports in a nearby park or spend your leisure time on or near a lake? You might choose a rural environment to avoid some measure of pollution. Would proximity to a strong medical community for good health care help you make a final choice?

Where you live affects your intellectual health in a few obvious ways. Your priority may be to choose a good school district. You may want to move to a college town even if no one in your family is in school, just for the general intellectual environment.

When you're balancing on the rent-or-buy seesaw, mental well-being factors in big time. Professional financial advisers probably won't tell you how much owning a home can be a royal pain. When you own, there are an awful lot of responsibilities beyond calling the landlord if something is amiss in your apartment. You might feel a great deal of mental anguish if you find yourself owning a home while in a job that is unstable. Losing your job in that context could be disastrous. For some people, worrying about real estate market instability is not worth the stress. What is the value of removing mental stress by taking on a more carefree renting situation?

As mentioned earlier, moving choices can often revolve around relationships. Are you moving closer to family or friends? You might be making tough decisions around which close friends will be neighbors and which will become long-distance connections.

Economic health, when choosing between renting and buying, is probably going to fuel the most complex conversations. Can you afford a down payment? What kind of loan makes the most sense? Who will be the guarantor of the loan?

Some mortgage underwriters analyze your debt-to-income ratio to see if you can afford payments, but this can be a false reading. They are looking at retrospective information—old jobs and old paychecks—but not future information. You are the one who knows what your future holds, even more than an underwriter. Will you be able to handle the payments?

Here is an important question that doesn't get much play: what's your exit strategy? And how long do you want to stay? You should know that at today's rates it would likely cost you 6 percent of the cost to sell the home, plus 2 to 5 percent for closing costs and improvements. It is reasonable to estimate sinking 10 percent of the cost of the home back in when you sell, so be sure to factor that into the mix.

Alternatively, what does it cost to rent in the same area? Can you find a property where the rent is not likely to skyrocket? The pros and cons in this economic category will probably weigh heavily on the decision.

Safety and risk management, in this case, are fairly straightforward.

How's the neighborhood? If you really love the culture of a certain area, would you be willing to put up with a slightly higher crime rate? Diligence and luck will hopefully turn up a spot for you with little risk and the right vibe.

Now it's time to make it real with our Integrative Decision Making system. Weigh the options and commit to what gives you the greatest ROI. Now sign at the bottom and call the moving van, and you've got yourself a new home.

THE COURAGE TO EXECUTE YOUR ROI DECISION

Through most of my life, I have not been afraid to take chances. My wife freaked out on vacation when I decided to go nighttime scuba diving off the coast of Maui. At a certain point, I realized the guide had lost track of me. I saw only watery blackness all around. Once I was out of the predicament, the whole thing seemed kind of funny. Leave it to me to get lost on a nighttime dive.

To celebrate the end of my first year of medical school, I jumped out of an airplane—static line skydiving. I may not be quite that brash anymore, but it was a blast at the time.

The high-risk lifestyle I've led at various points in my life can lend itself to high ROI rewards. Of course it can also lead to major crash and burn. If you happen to be more conservative when it comes to risk taking, safety in all its manifestations is probably high on your list of priorities. You should stick your neck out only so far for love or money. Your risk tolerance may fall somewhere in between. Either way, determining your risk tolerance gives you added information to help you go for the best of life's ROI in ways that work for you.

OBEY THE LAW OF DIMINISHING RETURNS

The examples of how to decide on a vacation and how to navigate the choices when finding a new home have helped us tackle quite a few ROI concepts. I'd like to introduce one more idea that will help tremendously as you come to understand and define your Core Asset allocation. It's the law of diminishing returns—one of the best-known laws in the world of economics. It tells us that in all productive processes, as you increase input of a single factor while other factors remain constant, your overall yield will begin to decrease. In laymen's terms, this means that when you continue to pour resources into something—even something wonderful and positive—at some point it will start to give back lower and lower positive returns, and eventually it will have a negative effect rather than a cumulative effect. In other words, there can indeed be too much of a good thing.

In finance, if you invest a given percentage of your funds in a single stock you know is performing well, you will likely get a very good return. If you double the percentage of your available funds and invest in that stock, you may still increase your returns. However, the amount of the increase may be less than double. If you were to invest even more, your overall return would grow incrementally at best. Eventually, if you were to keep going, all of your money would be riding on one company's stock performance, which is a formula for financial disaster. Financial advisers tell people to diversify for good reason. Diversifying and balancing your personal life also makes sense.

As it turns out, it works the same way in everyday life with all of our Core Assets. The law of diminishing returns can be portrayed as a curve (see Figure 2.1).

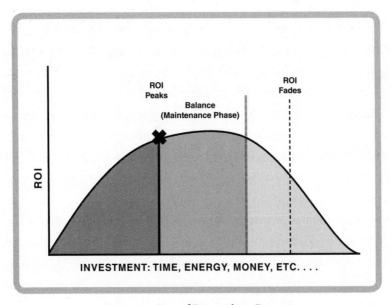

Figure 2.1. Law of Diminishing Returns

It's best to invest your currencies—time, energy, emotions, social, and money—in ways that maintain overall balance. Rather than giving too much and sliding down to where the curve indicates poor output, we want to do our best to stay in the sweet spot.

Let's take a look at some examples beyond the financial realm. How might the law of diminishing returns work for physical performance? Say you are training for a sports competition. In the early phases of your training, you work hard. You make great progress in building muscle, increasing flexibility, developing aerobic efficiency, and gaining overall stamina. You feel sure you are going to do your very best on the big day.

At some point, you feel that you are at peak performance; so even more training will catapult you beyond your very best, right?

Wrong. Instead you find you hit a plateau for a while, and then your performance worsens. Why? You have begun overtraining, which leads to a lack of proper resting periods. Your muscles don't have enough recovery time, and you put yourself at a higher risk for injuries. Pedal it back a bit, give your body time to recoup itself, and you will have a better chance at achieving excellence. That is, you can maximize your physical ROI.

You can visualize the curve pattern in the previous illustration to help find balance in Core Asset allocation when planning something specific, like training for a race, or in understanding how the balance works over time. In developing a spiritual life, for example, the beginning of the curve represents the increasing benefits of spirituality as your attentions are turned to its pursuit. There is self-discovery, personal growth, and increased understanding. At its peak there is a plateau of enlightenment and an overall sense of contentment.

If so much energy is put toward this one aspect that other parts of life are neglected or the intensity of the focus spills over into radicalism, the ROI decreases, as shown by a downturn on the curve. Remembering to attend to other parts of life in conjunction with spiritual consciousness will lead to an overall greater ROI on spirituality.

This pattern can fluctuate over a lifetime. In relationships, people often start on the upswing of discovering romantic interest and dating. They go on to reach heights with the perfect balance of love and friendship. The breakup of a long-term relationship causes a sharp downturn. As emotional healing, dating, and new relationships surface, the ascent toward a positive ROI begins anew.

There are countless good examples of how the law of diminishing returns works in everyday life. As we move through subsequent chapters, watch for more ways it comes into play as we encounter each of the Core Assets in more detail. Stay aware of this law while holding the overall vision of your current Core Asset allocation: That's a winning combination.

KEEP AHEAD OF THE GAME WITH CAPS

At the end of the upcoming chapter on each of the Core Assets defined by ASPIRES, you'll find a list of CAPS—Core Asset Protection Strategies. If you are training for that big race, one of the CAPS you might keep in mind is to take the slogan "no pain, no gain" only so far. Caring for your body in a mindful way protects your physical health asset. Listen to your body when it is sending an important signal and you'll stay on the sweet spot of the law of diminishing returns curve. That will give you a higher ROI, and that's the result we want.

Keep an eye out for the CAPS and let them be an extra guide on your journey through learning to balance your most important Assets: Safety, Physical, Intellectual, Relationships, Economic, and Spiritual.

As you can see, making a good decision isn't always an easy thing. Before this you might have looked at decision making like a some-assembly-required kids' toy with instructions in every language but yours. Now, however, you've got methods. Remember that no matter what any adviser or so-called expert tells you, you hold the key to making the best decisions for you. Use the Integrative Decision Making system, tease out what matters to you most by looking at it through the ASPIRES lens, and bring it all into focus.

The next several chapters will dive into each Core Asset in as much detail as possible. This will aid you in making some of the tough decisions in your life. Of course, this information will not be fully comprehensive. However, it should be enough to help start framing your decision making to maximize your ROI.

3

Hold on to Your Assets: Your ROI on Safety

A QUICK LOOK AT THE WORLD OF SAFETY

We have all heard of the old cliché, *safety first*. This is an area many of us take for granted and perhaps readily dismiss. Living a life being conscious of safety is what gives you the best shot at holding on to all those good things you have worked so hard to attain.

Let's think about safe driving. According to the Centers for Disease Control, motor vehicle accidents are the leading cause of death for people between the ages of five and thirty-four. Alcohol impairment and neglecting to use seatbelts are the main culprits. A simple act of texting while driving can instantly wipe your slate clean of all those assets you've worked so hard to attain. So, in reality, despite how hard you've worked on your dream house, despite the beautiful family you've raised with the love of your life, and despite how much money you've invested to finance your early retirement, if you make a quick, errant choice, all those beautiful assets could be wiped away in one terrible instant.

This isn't designed to scare you, but it is designed to make you think. If you're reading this book, you care about making the most of your life. Why take unnecessary risks that could throw it all away? So let's add safety to our list of Core Assets to give full value to this essential piece of the puzzle.

Safety is very broad in scope. It isn't possible to review all its various forms in this book. The list that follows outlines several areas of concern. Look for the ones with an asterisk (*) next to them discussed in this chapter and later.

A percentage of our tax dollars goes to agencies that work to enhance our safety in society, over which we don't necessarily have direct control. Auto, boat, and air traffic agencies help regulate a good portion of our transportation safety. We have standards that dictate work safety and mandate that employers be responsible for mitigating occupational risks by providing protective gear and suitable conditions for workers. Food, drugs, water, dairy, and consumer products are also regulated for safety purposes.

Intelligence agencies help prevent criminal and fraudulent activity and provide national defense to help protect our borders. Meanwhile firefighters and police operate as essential parts of our outsourced safety network within our local neighborhoods. All these forms of safety are essential for a healthy, well-organized society.

For our purposes here, we will discuss the kinds of safety you can

Environmental

Air pollution (indoor/ outdoor)

Arsenic

Asbestos

Biological hormones

Carbon monoxide

DDT

Electrical and magnetic fields

Hazardous wastes

Lead

Mercury

Ozone

Pesticides

Radiation (X-rays, nuclear, cosmic, solar)

Water pollution

Health and Medical Safety

Cancer risks*

Communicable diseases (TB, HIV)

Drug resistance

Medical devices (implants, meshes, surgical devices)

Obesity (diabetes, heart disease, hypertension, stroke risks)*

Prescription drug abuse (polypharmacy, overdose, medical errors)*

Preventive medical health screening*

Public health (vaccines, epidemics)

Sexually transmitted diseases (STDs)

Vaccines and immunizations

Home, Work, Transportation

Accidents (falls, home tools, kitchen and grill)

Cyber safety*

Ergonomics (carpal tunnel, lumbar support)

Financial safety*

Firearms safety

Fire safety

Food safety

Identity theft*

Motor vehicle safety (airbags, sobriety, distractions such as texting and talking on cell phones)

National security (terrorism, national defense, border security)

Occupational safety (eye and hand protection)

Public safety

Sports and exercise safety*

Transportation safety (aircraft, boating, public railways/subways)

Vices (alcohol, tobacco, recreational drugs)*

Water safety

work to control and maximize in your own life. Let's take a look at some of the things you can do to get the very best ROI on safety.

KEEP AN EYE ON YOUR HEALTH WITH PREVENTIVE SCREENINGS

Remembering to get your regular checkup might not be the first thing you think of when you consider living a safer life. In fact, getting a checkup at all can be easily overlooked. When you're young, you feel good and don't think you need to see a doctor. Most of us are leading busy lives. Who has time for health screenings?

The truth is we all ought to make time. Getting used to regular health screenings sets the foundation for your future well-being. The older we get, the more critical it becomes.

During one of my routine physicals I found out I had high cholesterol and my vitamin D level was well below normal limits. I admit I used to be in that category of carefree people who didn't think much about checkups. I'm grateful I got over it and took care of it. By being health conscious, I was able to recognize the importance of diet and exercise to complete the health equation. Even a routine vision screening while updating my glasses prescription proved to be a surprise. During a routine screening test while at my appointment I was suspected of having glaucoma. Fortunately it turned out to be a false alarm. But the scare still had an effect—it raised my awareness of the possibility. Things can and do go wrong with our bodies. It is far safer to discover a problem early, while there's still ample time to correct it.

When you consider how and where you should go to get your health care, there are many choices available. The most common is conventional, allopathic medicine (MD). Other disciplines include osteopathy (DO), podiatry (DPM), chiropractic (DC), dentistry (DMD), optometry (OD), naturopathic (ND), and ayurvedic medicine, to name a few. Ayurveda in particular is near and dear to me because my late grandfather practiced it for more than fifty years. Ayurveda is a traditional system from India that works with dietary recommendations, herbal preparations, and other elements to generate healing and balance. It has yet to take a foothold in the Western world mainly due to lack of regulation and safety concerns over some of the herbal formulations.

Whichever health pathway you choose, be sure these disciplines are complementary rather than contradictory. There can be drug interactions with concurrent use of some herbal supplements and conventional medicines, so make sure your health professional is aware of everything you are taking.

Regardless of your preference, health screenings should never be disregarded. I know that's easier said than done. Sometimes simple procrastination or anxiety about medical procedures keeps people away from their doctors. Other times real financial burdens, lack of insurance, and related factors stop people from getting necessary screenings. Unfortunately that means some people who've been skipping their screenings are walking around with ticking time bombs inside them. When that is the case, it is a sad fact that by the time a health problem is discovered, it is usually too late.

This is where the economic Core Asset meets the physical health Core Asset. Without enough financial resources, the physical Core Asset may be neglected. Collectively it is more of an economic burden on society to deal with the aftermath of diagnosis and advanced disease than to deal with the upfront costs of early detection and prevention. Health screening awareness is a step in the right direction.

Then it must be seen all the way through, with timely intervention and compliance.

Here is some additional information on health routines that will help keep you, and all of us, safer.

BLOOD SCREENING

Laboratory testing of blood should be done routinely. Keeping an eye on your cholesterol level as well as your fasting blood sugar can help you turn around potential major ailments before they have a chance to take hold. Your fasting blood sugar test should be done at least every three years. If you are at a higher risk for diabetes, take the test annually.

Cholesterol testing should be done every five years after age thirty-five in men and forty-five in women. If you have extra risk factors, starting sooner is recommended—even as early as age twenty. The A1C test measures average blood sugar control over the past two to three months. Since this is an average, it is not subject to fluctuations in sugar levels during different times of the day.

C-reactive protein (CRP) is released by the liver when there is inflammation in the body. It can be a reliable indicator of the potential for sudden heart attack or stroke. If you have CRP levels greater than 3mg/L, you are at high risk. You would also be at increased risk of getting diabetes and high blood pressure. Exercise can reduce it by up to 35 percent.

Homocysteine is derived from a breakdown of methionine, an amino acid. It's a marker for an unhealthy lifestyle and goes up when you have a diet high in saturated and trans fats. It also goes up with excessive smoking and alcohol.

VISION SCREENING AND EYE CARE

They say the eyes are the windows to the soul. Unfortunately, many of us take these windows for granted. The eyes should be cared for throughout life. Between the ages of eighteen and forty, an eye exam is recommended every two years. If you have a family history of diabetes or eye disease, a yearly exam would be more prudent.

Protecting your eyes from UV radiation is very important. Too much UV radiation can actually cause sunburn of the eye, a temporary but unpleasant condition called photokeratitis. Long-term overexposure to UV becomes increasingly dangerous—cataracts, macular degeneration, and moles in the back of the eye that eventually lead to melanomas may result. Sunglasses, then, are a must. Don't buy any that don't tell you specifically what they can do for you beyond make you look cool. They should be able to screen out 99 percent of UVA and UVB rays and 75 to 90 percent of visible light.

But wait, there's more. You can even protect your vision by paying attention to what you eat. Eye-friendly foods include green, leafy vegetables as well as eggs, which contain lutein and zeaxanthin. Try adding some broccoli, spinach, peas, turnip greens, and collards into your diet to take in your share of these carotenoids. They are considered protective against age-related macular degeneration and cataracts, both of which are leading causes of visual impairment and blindness among older individuals.

DENTAL HEALTH AND ORAL HYGIENE

Many health plans don't include dental care, which may lead some people to believe it is not important. This is not the case. Practicing good oral hygiene not only benefits your teeth and gums but also can actually do a lot to raise your overall ROI on health and safety from bacterial infections and even heart disease.

Most people know this, but it bears repeating: it is important to brush after every meal, or a minimum of two times daily. Plaque is a key component of dental disease, and it is mainly the toothbrush, not the toothpaste, that does the work to battle it. Choose a toothbrush with soft bristles made of nylon. Try not to use too much pressure, since aggressive brushing may actually erode the enamel. Note that the natural color of our teeth is not actually white. Slightly yellow or even a light reddish tone is very normal, so there is no need to over-brush in an attempt to uncover a Hollywood smile.

Remember to brush your gums so as not to get cavities starting at the gum's edge. Although you should use fluoride toothpaste, fluoride is actually more effective when taken internally through fluoridated water than when applied topically.

Floss daily. An irrigating device may be helpful to loosen debris, stimulate gums, and promote balance by diluting toxins and acids in the mouth. And don't forget your regular checkups every six months.

If you have chronic bad odors in the mouth, lozenges, gum, and most mouthwashes are usually not very helpful. This condition may indicate an underlying digestive problem. If you notice bad breath, take it as a cue to screen for other potential health issues.

Various medical societies and health agencies make recommendations regarding when to be screened and for which health markers. Figure 3.1 will give you an overview. I encourage you to take a look, mark your calendar, and make those appointments.

	Screening	Purpose	20–29	30–39	40–49	50–59	60+
GENERAL	Cholesterol, HDL, LDL, and triglycerides	Identify people at high risk for coronary artery disease	Every 5 years depending on level	Every 5 years depending on level	Every 1–3 years depending on level	Annually	Annually
	EKG	Identify injury to heart or irregular rhythms			Baseline test between ages 40 and 45	Annually	Annually
	General Physical Exam	Detect conditions before symptoms develop	Every 2–3 years	Every 2–3 years	Every 2–3 years	Annually	Annually
	Immunizations	Create immunity against a particular disease	Diphtheria–Tetanus every 10 years. Rubella once if necessary (females only). Influenza annually age 65 and older, Pneumococcalvaccine once after age 65.				
	Rectal Exam	Detect any abnormalities in the rectum				Annually	Annually
	Colonoscopy	Detect cancers and growths (polyps) on the inside wall of the colon before they become cancerous				Baseline test at 50, then every 5–10 years	Every 5–10 years
	Hemoccult	Detect blood in stool to screen for various diseases				Annually	Annually
	General Eye Exam	Detect hidden disease processes in the eye or body as a whole	Every 5–10 years	Every 5–10 years	Every 3–5 years	Every 3 years	Every 1–2 years
WOMEN	Breast Self-Exam	Look for color changes, skin irregularities, lumps, and changes in the nipples	Monthly	Monthly	Monthly	Monthly	Monthly
	Mammography	Detect cancer and precancerous changes			Baseline test at 40	Annually	Annually
	Pap Smear	Detect abnormal cells that may become cancerous	Annually	Every 1–3 years	Every 1–3 years	Every 1–3 years	Every 1–3 years
	Pelvic Exam	Detect cancer and precancerous changes of the cervix, uterus, and ovaries	Annually	Annually	Annually	Annually	Annually
	Bone Density Screening	Detect osteoporosis and bone thinning					Baseline test at 60
MEN	Prostate-Specific Antigen	Detect prostate cancer in the earliest stages				Annually	Annually
	Testicular Self-Exam	Detect testicular cancer, the most common malignancy in American men between ages 15 and 35	Monthly	Monthly	Monthly	Monthly	Monthly
	Digital Rectal Exam	Identify an early growth or tumor in the prostate gland				Annually	Annually

These are overall guidelines and should not be construed as a medical recommendation or a substitution for medical advice.

Figure 3.1. Personal Health Screening Guidelines

AT-HOME HEALTH CHECKS

There are certainly things that are best left to professionals when it comes to your health care, but there is also a lot you can do on your own to strive for maximum ROI on health-related safety. Make self-screening part of your routine. Monthly breast self-exams, testicular self-exams, monitoring your heart rate and blood pressure, and keeping an eye on your weight and skin are just a few of the things you can do yourself.

BLOOD PRESSURE

Yours can vary quite a bit; so don't get too upset if it seems unusually high or low on occasion or during a particular part of the day. Blood pressure rises normally after a salty diet, caffeine, exercise, exposure to cold, or if you've taken any type of drug that can affect it. It is okay to take your blood pressure at any time of day, but it is best to check it again at that same time daily for consistent readings. Your doctor may also ask you to take your blood pressure at different times to monitor fluctuation throughout the day.

There are many good devices on the market for checking blood pressure. The World Health Organization (WHO) and the International Society of Hypertension (ISH) have developed the blood pressure chart/classification in Figure 3.2 as a guide to what is high and what is normal blood pressure.

If you find that you are consistently out of the normal range, notify your doctor so he or she may make an analysis for potential causes.

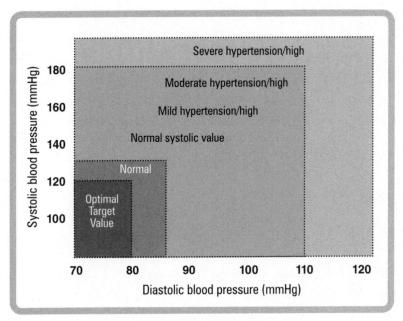

Figure 3.2. Blood Pressure Classifications

Source: Classification by the World Health Organization/International Society of Hypertension.

HEART RATE

There are two main places on the body where you can check the heart rate. The first is found on your wrist, just below your thumb. This is where you will find your radial pulse. You can also feel for your carotid pulse in your neck. Either way, press very lightly with your index and middle fingers. Once you feel the pulse, it is ideal to count it over a period of one minute. If you are impatient, it is also acceptable to take the measurement by counting the pulse for fifteen seconds and multiplying the number by four. A normal heart rate for someone at rest and under the age of eighteen is seventy to one hundred beats per minute. For those over eighteen, the resting heart rate range is sixty to one hundred.

It is also very useful to monitor your heart rate during exercise: Calculate your maximum heart rate by taking 220 and subtracting your age. Your target heart rate for fat-burning and cardio exercise will range from 60 to 85 percent of your maximum heart rate.

GENDER-SPECIFIC SCREENING

MEN

For males, prostate screenings should start at age fifty. This would include a DRE (digital rectal exam) performed by your physician as well as a colonoscopy screening for colon cancer. I know it sounds a bit daunting, but at least it's not an everyday thing. In addition, men can do their own at-home testicular self-exams, looking for unusual lumps, heaviness, or enlargement.

WOMEN

Current guidelines established by the National Cancer Institute recommend that women should have a Pap test every three years beginning at age twenty-one. These guidelines further recommend that women ages thirty to sixty-five should have HPV and Pap cotesting every five years, or a Pap test alone every three years. Women with certain risk factors may need to have more frequent screenings or continue screenings beyond age sixty-five.

Women should perform breast self-exams monthly. It is recommended that women who are still menstruating do this self-check a few days after their periods end. A breast self-exam may be done by looking in a mirror, in the shower, or in a lying down position. Use your hand in a reasonably firm circular motion to get to know what your normal breast tissue feels like so you can recognize changes. By the way, don't worry if one breast is larger than the other. A little asymmetry is normal and is actually quite common. It is important to watch for lumps, discoloration, areas of skin thickening, puckering or dimpling, or discharge from the nipple such as blood or pus. Most cancers are found under the nipple or near the armpit. If any of these abnormalities are discovered, it is very important to get to your doctor right away for further testing. It is recommended women in their twenties have clinical breast exams (CBEs) about every three years, and every year for women forty and over.

There is a bit of controversy about mammograms for breast cancer screening. The American Cancer Society recommends yearly mammograms starting at age forty. However, some advocates favor starting at age fifty. If you have a high risk factor such as breast cancer in the family, the sooner you make mammograms a routine part of your annual wellness plan the better—perhaps even before the guidelines recommend.

SKIN SAFETY

The skin is the largest organ of the body. It is our primary defense against bacteria and toxins, and a cooling mechanism via our sweat glands; it promotes vitamin D production, guards against dehydration, and does our bodies a great service through its role in healing wounds. This is a part of us that needs attention and care.

As I was growing up, I had to learn firsthand about skin care. I had a fairly intense case of teenage acne, and the dermatologist I saw gave me some fairly heavy-duty medications that caused sun sensitivity. Extra caution and sunscreen was of utmost importance;

without them I might have experienced a negative impact on my skin that may have lasted to this day.

The aspects of sunlight that do most of the damage to skin are the two forms of ultraviolet radiation—UVA and UVB. The light frequencies we are able to see have a wavelength of 400 to 760 nm and do not cause skin damage. The UVA wavelength ranges from 320 to 400 nm and penetrates the skin, causing deep tissue damage. UVB, at 290 to 320 nm, is the one that causes sunburn. Both may be cancer causing.

If you think you don't need sunscreen, you're wrong. You do. Look for an SPF (sun protection factor) of fifteen at minimum. Those with fairer skin types—like type I (usually found on redheads) and type II (common on blondes with blue eyes)—should use at least SPF thirty. It is best to apply your sunscreen thirty minutes before sun exposure. And yes, cloudy days count. Even on a cloudy day, 80 percent of the UV rays get through.

Be generous with your sunscreen—use at least one ounce over the entire body once every one to two hours at minimum. Don't buy into waterproof sunscreen. There really is no such thing. Just remember to reapply after water exposure or towel drying. Remember to replace sunscreen that has passed its expiration date, and store it in a cool place, as heat, over time, will degrade the product.

You should cover every part of you that will be exposed to the sun, including your ears and extremities. Your lips should also be covered with a lip balm with SPF. Lipsticks often have an SPF of about five, which is not enough. Look for a lip balm that has an SPF of twenty or more.

Your clothing can also work to protect your skin. The average T-shirt has an SPF of only four, but you can buy products that raise the SPF level of your clothes up to thirty. They are usually good for twenty to thirty washings before reapplication is necessary.

The reason for all of these protective measures is to prevent skin cancer, one of the most commonly diagnosed diseases, particularly in North America and parts of Europe. While sunscreen is a necessary form of protection, sun avoidance can be a good idea in some cases as well. If you have type I or type II skin or are particularly sun sensitive, consider avoiding being out and about between 11:00 a.m. and 3:00 p.m., when UV rays are at their highest. People of all skin types should be vigilant about skin self-screening. Get to know the texture and markings on your skin. Notice any changes.

Basal cell carcinoma appears as a nonhealing sore or sometimes as a pinkish growth or bump. It is most often seen on the neck or face, or around the nose. Squamous cell carcinoma typically appears on the head and neck and has a scar-like appearance.

Melanoma is the most common cancer found among people in their twenties. Some have a genetic predisposition for developing it. It is common to find melanoma on the back in men, and on the lower leg in women. It appears black and irregular, generally with rough edges.

If you don't know whether a change in appearance of your skin is suspicious or not, be on the safe side and see your doctor.

MINDING YOUR P'S: POOP, PEE, AND POOT

Well, we've just gone through several types of self-screening designed to keep you safer through early detection of disease or pre-disease conditions. There is another series of personal screenings you can do. They don't get much attention, probably because of the stigma associated with them. It is an area that can draw private snickers and public jeers. The jokes and awkward feelings can cut across all ages and cultures.

Yes, evaluating these bodily emissions can indeed give you clues about your well-being. It is worth the effort for you to start to notice what your body releases as waste, and any changes that might take place. Once you get past any squeamishness, you might be surprised by what you can learn about your health.

POOP

Okay, perhaps we need to get some of the expected bathroom humor out of the way. Our first P, poop, has other English names as well, such as dump, turd, and crap, just to name a few. In Hindi the word is *tati*. In Italy they say *cacca*, similar to the Spanish term *caca*. In Dutch it's *schijt*.

On a more serious note, stool can be a pretty good indicator of your GI health. Normal stool is about 75 percent water, and it is usually brown because the bile released from the gall bladder mixed with intestinal contents and bacteria creates that color. Taking certain supplements or medications can change stool color. Iron can make it green or black, and antibiotics can turn it blackish as well. If it is orange, you likely had a diet high in beta carotene, which would have included carrots, pumpkins, and vitamin A supplements.

If it is consistently very pale, this could indicate a gall bladder or bile dysfunction. If you see red stool or stool that is streaked or spotted with red, you are likely experiencing bleeding in the colon. You may have hemorrhoids or tears in the colon. Notify your doctor immediately. A continual lower GI bleed can be life threatening.

Hard stool can indicate a form of dehydration. Hard, black stools are a strong indicator of upper GI bleeding, as this may mean any blood present has had time to change from red to black. This could be coming from the esophagus, a bleeding stomach ulcer, or an intestinal ulcer.

Some colon cancers can narrow the passageway to create pencil-thin stools. Inflammatory bowel disease can do this also. Notify your doctor if you suspect these conditions.

If your stool is slimy or mucus-covered, or has pus, it might be indicative of a food allergy, an infection, or a parasite. If it's greasy and smelly, it may mean you have too much fat in your diet, or you are not absorbing fat properly. If it tends to float, there may be excessive gas present. This might indicate celiac disease (i.e. difficulty in digesting gluten, a component of wheat and other grains).

It is also useful to notice how often you move your bowels. Once or twice a day is typical, and the amount usually ranges from three to eight ounces. You should be able to go without straining too hard. If you are straining, you are at a greater risk for hemorrhoids and anal fissures as well as a condition called diverticulosis. Colon cancer risk also goes up due to lack of fiber in the diet. Constipation may indicate you need to take in more fluids in your diet to ward off dehydration.

PEE

Our second P—pee, or piss—is a commonly used English term for urination. The normal color of pee is light yellow to dark amber. In the absence of any supplements that may turn it a deep yellow, the darker it is, the more dehydrated you are. If there's no color, you may actually be overhydrated.

If your urine has a black hue, it could be due to certain medications. Eating a generous amount of fava beans or rhubarb can have the same result. Orange may be the result of medications, laxatives, or beta carotene in your diet. While it may certainly be surprising, if your pee comes out blue it is not a cause for alarm. This odd color is usually the result of blue dye that is an additive in some medications. However, if you see red or even pink urine, call your doctor immediately. Blood in the urine is a major warning sign, and you must be evaluated.

Several conditions are indicative of a possible urinary tract infection (UTI). Cloudy and/or smelly urine could point to a UTI. If you are experiencing a burning sensation and have to pee frequently, these could also be indicative of an infection. However, frequent urination is a symptom of other problems as well. If you have to go too often, especially at night, diabetes could be indicated. In men it could be a symptom of an abnormally enlarged prostate.

Tea-colored urine is a symptom of dehydration, but it could also indicate a more serious condition: the breakdown of muscle. This condition is found primarily in athletes and people on cholesterol medication, and can be life threatening.

POOT

Finally, our last P is poot, or fart. Yes, this topic gets more than its share of giggles out of everyone's inner child. A polite way to put it in the United States is passing gas. Sometimes we also call it breaking wind, dropping a stink bomb, or cutting the cheese. It's *furz* in Germany, it's *pud* in Hindi, *peto* in Italian, *fang* in Cantonese, and *nuhfeechal* in Israeli.

Did you know that 20 percent of the methane emissions in the world are due to the farts of cows and other livestock? But the average person passes gas once an hour, for a total of one to three pints of gas each day. A combination of oxygen, nitrogen, and carbon dioxide is released each time, which can recombine to form methane or hydrogen. When someone lights a match in the bathroom, those are the gases that can light up.

Smelly gas usually has high sulfur content, or there may be a high level of bacteria. Certain foods can also contribute to the odor, particularly broccoli, cauliflower, cabbage, onions, garlic, eggs, and dairy products.

Frequent farting could indicate lactose intolerance. In this case the lactase enzyme usually present to break down the sugar lactose is missing, and excess gas and sometimes discomfort are the result. Passing gas with frequency may also point to food allergies or sensitivities.

Even though there is no end to the jokes and fun we can make of this topic, it has a more serious side. These are natural and necessary functions. In the privacy of your own home, you can learn to evaluate the waste you release. Let it help you recognize changes and signs of any health matters that may arise.

AVOID THE ADDICTIONS

We all want to have fun and enjoy life. There is absolutely nothing wrong with a drink now and then as part of that. However, the extent to which overuse and abuse of drugs, alcohol, and tobacco generates a poor ROI on life really cannot be overstated. What starts out as social and recreational use can quickly become extremely destructive. For safety's sake, set limits, or recognize it is best to avoid these substances all together.

SHRUG OFF THE DRUG

I have witnessed the use and dangerous effects of illicit drugs during and beyond my college years as well as during my medical training. I trained near some of the roughest communities in the United States, blocks from the infamous 8 Mile Road in Detroit and within South Central, Los Angeles—the heart of the gang wars between the Crips and the Bloods. Being up close to the drug use environment and its associated side effects, such as severe withdrawal symptoms and the violence it sparked, was truly unnerving.

No matter how good it may feel initially, when drug use becomes an addiction, it can severely damage the body and brain. Rather than moralize or shame someone who has gotten caught in the web of drug addiction, I would rather offer ways to help understand the problem and let people know it is possible to find help and remove this toxic hazard from their lives.

Abuse happens with both recreational drugs and prescription drugs. Recreational drug abuse used to be more common. While the reverse is currently true, here are some common recreational drugs and the trouble they can cause:

- **Marijuana** can worsen asthmatic conditions, bring about chronic coughing, weaken the immune system, and make you more susceptible to pneumonia and other infections. Yes, I am well aware of its proposed medicinal use, especially for those with chronic pain. A deeper understanding along with clinical guidelines needs to be established to prevent its misuse.

- **Cocaine** can increase the heart rate and blood pressure to dangerous levels. Sudden heart attacks as a result of this drug are quite common.

- **Opioids** like heroin can slow the heart rate and reduce the breathing rate to dangerously low and sometimes fatal levels.

- **Methamphetamines** can cause prolonged insomnia, hyperthermia, irregular heartbeats, paranoia, aggressiveness, and eventually, cardiovascular collapse.

- **Hallucinogens** include substances like LSD and psilocybin mushrooms. They can cause people to think, hear, and see things that don't exist or aren't happening, possibly leading to disastrous results.

- **Inhalants** are anything used by breathing in fumes, such as amyl nitrate, gasoline, anesthetics like nitrous oxide, hairsprays, bug sprays, bath salts, and other types of solvents. The physical and psychological damage done by these vary by substance, and it seems obvious that gasoline, bug spray, and the like were never intended to be inhaled in any amount.

If you find that you or someone you love has a drug problem, seeking help in an inpatient facility is often a very good idea. The first step to getting off drugs is detoxification, and in most cases it is a difficult ride. When the body rids itself of the drug or drugs in the system, the process can trigger withdrawal symptoms such as restlessness, insomnia, diarrhea, vomiting, depression, hysteria, and other painful, frightening maladies. By checking into a facility during the first days and weeks of getting clean, a person can be closely monitored and helped to cope with the symptoms of withdrawal, which can last hours or days, and then with the psychological struggle and changes that often follow.

PRESCRIPTION MEDS: USE BUT DON'T ABUSE

Currently, prescription drugs are the most commonly abused type of drugs among youths, especially twelve- and thirteen-year-olds. However, they are now even more commonly abused among adults since they are easily obtained. Even some over-the-counter drugs like pseudoephedrine, diet pills, and cough syrup have become popular highs, or their ingredients are used to make more complex addictive substances. There is a misperception that these are safer than illegal street drugs. The increasing use of drugs for uses other than their intended purposes has led to an associated rise in addiction, accidents, and other maladies. We hear a lot of messages today about avoiding drunk driving, but people need to recognize that drugged driving is equally dangerous.

In recent years there has been an increase in deaths specifically from painkiller abuse. Commonly abused painkillers include Vicodin, methadone, Darvocet, Percocet, and Oxycontin. In the United States it has been reported that more than fifteen million people have abused prescription drugs. That's more than the combined users of heroin, cocaine, inhalants, and hallucinogens. The problem is also growing in other regions, including Europe, South Asia, and South Africa. Although they are tragedies, celebrity deaths like those of Michael Jackson and Whitney Houston increase awareness and shed some light on the dangers of prescription drugs.

Some of the signs of prescription drug abuse are: mood swings, changes in personality, reduced concentration, lack of energy, and social withdrawal. Other things to look out for are defensiveness, blackouts and forgetfulness, sensitivity to lights and sounds, hallucinations, neglect of responsibilities, changes in daily habits and appearance, increased time and effort in trying to obtain prescriptions, progression of usage, and continual use beyond original medical conditions.

With this and other types of addiction, there are support groups out there to help those who are affected. First, individuals must recognize that they have a problem. When a commitment to treat the problem follows, real recovery can occur.

LOSE THE BOOZE

In some ways it is a little harder to recognize a potential problem with drinking as opposed to drugs. Although in many circles, the use of street drugs or pharmaceuticals is frowned upon, drinking alcohol is seen as no big deal. How do you know when it's too much and you've begun to lower your ROI on safety?

Everyone's body weight and tolerance to alcohol is a little different, but here are some basic rules to help you stay within limits:

- A standard drink is considered to be one beer, or one glass of wine, or one shot of liquor. Are any of these safer than the others? No. Each contains about half an ounce of alcohol.

- For a woman, one drink daily is considered moderate drinking. Drinking too much equals having three or more daily, or a drink a day over a seven- to thirty-day period, which is considered heavy drinking.

- For a man, two or fewer drinks per day is considered moderate drinking. Drinking too much equals having four or more drinks per day, or two drinks per day over a seven- to thirty-day period, which is considered heavy drinking.

- Five or more drinks for men or women on any one occasion is considered binge drinking.

If you find yourself or someone you know in a heavy drinking or binge drinking area, try to stay aware and steer yourself out of the danger zone. Despite its popularity and general acceptance, overuse of alcohol can be powerfully destructive and just as addictive as drugs. If there is alcoholism in your family, the risk is higher. Heavy drinking can damage the liver, pancreas, brain, and heart, and increase the risk of certain types of cancer. Women who drink during pregnancy risk causing birth defects. The possibility of accidents with machinery and in vehicles increases astronomically when you are under the influence of alcohol.

The signs of alcohol abuse include: having a strong craving to drink, not being able to limit intake, and increasing tolerance so that greater amounts continue to be needed to achieve the same effect. Physical dependency on alcohol may produce symptoms including nausea, shakiness, and anxiety when drinking is stopped. Just as the symptoms of drug abuse translate well into the symptoms associated with alcohol abuse, common signs of alcohol abuse and alcoholism might also show up in someone who is taking drugs, so it is best to be aware that when behaviors change in these directions, either or both might be a problem.

Just as there are facilities and programs for people addicted to narcotics and other drugs, you can also find help for problems with alcohol. Alcoholics Anonymous has changed the lives of many people for the better, and it is one of many pathways to sobriety.

Some research shows that in the absence of a problem with alcoholism, a little bit of alcohol is not bad for you. One glass of red wine is actually heart-friendly. Drinking socially in a controlled fashion is fine as long as you don't exceed limits or allow your judgment to become impaired—most especially while driving. Don't wipe out your high ROI on every other Core Asset by forgetting this very serious fact.

THE GREAT SMOKE OUT

Last but certainly not least, we have to take a look at the very poor ROI on tobacco use. Whether it's smoking cigarettes or cigars or chewing tobacco, the negative effects of this practice are staggering. Problems begin with chronic coughing, sore throat, stained teeth, mouth sores, gum deterioration, chronic bad breath, and increased risk of lung and oral cancers. Other medical side effects are elevated blood pressure, increased cholesterol, increased heart rate, stomach ulcers, and acid reflux. Smoking puts people around you at risk due to secondhand smoke.

I don't want to be morbid about it, but the list of ailments caused by tobacco use just keeps going. There aren't only lung and oral cancers to worry about. There is also an increased risk of esophageal, kidney, and bladder cancers, as well as stomach cancer and pancreatic cancer. If you smoke, your risk of heart attack or stroke increases by as much as four times over nonsmokers because smoking damages the lining of the heart and blood vessels. It can also increase the risk of lung diseases like chronic obstructive pulmonary disease (COPD), emphysema, and bronchitis. Smoking makes you more prone to sickness in general, including pneumonia and other infections. It also makes you appear to age much more quickly.

Nicotine is an extremely addictive drug. It can be just as addictive as heroin or cocaine, so it is very difficult to quit. Some people may believe taking smokeless tobacco is somehow healthier, but in reality more nicotine gets into the bloodstream that way than through smoking. These so-called pastimes are perceived as stress relievers, but there are so many other healthful ways to relieve stress.

The good news about quitting is that the short-term benefits begin immediately. According to the Centers for Disease Control, within twenty-three minutes of stopping, your blood pressure begins to improve. Oxygen intake increases because carbon monoxide in the blood is reduced. Therefore, in only twenty-four hours, your chance of a heart attack is decreased. After those twenty-four hours, you stop smelling like a smoker. In forty-eight hours, your nerves tend to recover, and your senses of taste and smell also improve. After seventy-two hours, the nicotine toxin is essentially cleared from the body, and breathing becomes much easier.

Those are short-term benefits, but stick with it—good news keeps on coming. In two to twelve weeks, your heart and lungs start to work better than before. Nine months free from smoking can reduce your rate of coughing and shortness of breath. After a year, your risk of heart disease is reduced by half. Ten years out: your risk of lung cancer is reduced by half. After fifteen years, you are back to the normal risk of heart disease and stroke as compared to a non-smoker. Those are the long-term effects of quitting.

By quitting smoking you significantly improve your ROI and can affect other Core Assets in very positive ways. All addictions are difficult to handle, but it can be done. It takes commitment to make the change. Support and encouragement from the people around you can be key.

There are medications that may help you break the nicotine

habit. The U.S. Food and Drug Administration has approved seven medications to aid in quitting smoking. Nicotine patches, nicotine gum, and nicotine lozenges are available over the counter, and a nicotine nasal spray and inhaler are currently available by prescription. Buproprion SR (Zyban) and varenicline (Chantix) are non-nicotine pills.

Once you have stopped smoking you could experience a relapse, but that doesn't mean you should stop trying. Most relapses happen in the first couple of months. Withdrawal symptoms are strongest in the initial phases of quitting but will lessen drastically in the first two weeks if you stick with it. During this time it is best to avoid alcohol and other people who smoke. Don't be surprised if you gain a little weight, perhaps even up to 10 pounds. Don't let that be a discouraging sign; let it be encouraging because with quitting, the net positive will be well worth any temporary weight gain. Eat healthfully and stay physically active, and you will be on the right track.

THE SAFER WORKOUT

We've already addressed fitness and exercise, but it bears revisiting to emphasize safety. When I first started getting more active, I would take a shotgun approach to it without knowing what I was doing. I would overdo things that would actually wind up hindering my progress. With weightlifting I didn't know about the true process of breathing and developed sports hernias, which required two surgeries to repair.

Before you get into your workout, start off in the safest way possible—with a health history and a physical exam by your physician, to make sure you are ready to embark on the program. There could be a preexisting issue like a heart condition or something else that could be made worse by changing or increasing physical activity. Make sure any medications you're taking aren't in conflict with your exercise program so you won't raise your heart rate and blood pressure to dangerous levels.

Here are some other basic tips to stay safe while you get fit:

- **Have the right gear.** Make sure your sports equipment and clothing are correct for the activities you're taking on. Especially for runners and walkers, have shoes that fit well. Otherwise you can create chronic foot problems that hinder the consistency of your exercise. Avoid rubber or plastic suits or belts, as these restrict proper cooling of the body.

- **Protect yourself.** That means wear a helmet for biking, knee pads for skating, elbow pads for high-impact sports, and the like. Wear a sports bra, athletic supporter, or other sex-appropriate protection as needed. If you think you look dorky wearing a helmet or other protective gear, get over it in the name of living to play another day in good health.

- **Light up the night.** Reflective clothing and other forms of light are important when running, walking, biking, or taking part in some other sport after dark.

- **Block the sun.** If you are going to be out in the sun, use sunglasses and, when possible, wear a hat. Sunscreen is a must. It is possible to get sunburn in the winter as well, so don't forget your SPF.

- **Dress for the weather.** Weather-appropriate clothing is important. Dressing in layers helps; you can remove layers as you start to sweat. Remaining dressed too warmly may cause dangerous levels of dehydration. In warmer weather, loose-fitting cotton in a light color is ideal. In cold weather, cotton is not recommended to be closest to your skin; try a synthetic like polypropylene instead. Protect your hands, feet, and ears when it is cold because blood first travels from these places to your core, leaving them most vulnerable to frostbite. Watch for high and low temperatures as well as wind chill, and avoid the extremes altogether, if possible.

- **Hydrate**. Drinking enough water before and during exercise is extremely important. Exercising while dehydrated is dangerous. You're likely to turn in a poor performance, too.

- **Know the summer weather risks**. Exercising in hot temperatures poses particular risks. First, be acclimated to the weather. As your body gets used to warmer temperatures, you may choose to increase the intensity of your workouts gradually.

  Second, be aware of the signs of heat cramps, heat exhaustion, and heat stroke. With heat cramps there are painful contractions in the calves, quadriceps, and abdomen, but the body temperature remains normal. With heat exhaustion the body temperature rises to 104 degrees Fahrenheit, or 40 degrees Celsius, which can be accompanied by vomiting, nausea, headaches, weakness, fainting, and clammy skin. If left untreated this can lead to heat stroke, which is an emergency condition. The body heats up above 104 degrees and cannot stop sweating in an attempt to cool itself. You may become delirious, confused, and irritable. Brain damage, organ failure, and even death may follow without treatment.

- **Learn your sport.** Get to know the proper way to perform your workout or play the sport of your choice. Technique and form are very important to prevent injury. Don't hesitate to seek expert advice if need be.

- **Don't overdo it.** In the enthusiasm to start a new exercise program, a lot of people—myself very much included—may tend to overexercise. Taking on too much too soon, or going too fast for too long, leads to overuse injuries like strained muscles and even sprains and bone injuries. Crosstraining—taking on an activity that's not part of your primary routine or sports goal—varies the routine and helps balance muscle groups so you are not overemphasizing a particular body area. Whatever you do, remember to pace yourself.

Even with your best efforts, you still may suffer an injury. If you do, one of the smartest and safest things you can do is treat it with RICE: Rest, Ice, Compression, and Elevation.

You should first rest the injured part for forty-eight hours. Apply ice in some form—cold pack, a bag of crushed ice, or whatever is convenient—for twenty minutes at a time, four to eight times per day. Use compression by putting pressure on the area to reduce swelling. Elastic wraps, air casts, and splints all serve this purpose. Finally, elevation keeps the injured part above the level of the heart. It may be as simple as using a pillow to prop up an injured limb.

You can use RICE to treat an injury rapidly. In severe cases, get medical care, especially if there is a fracture, dislocation, or any prolonged pain or swelling. Yes, even I have started icing up my joints a bit now and then.

IDENTITY THEFT AND CYBER SECURITY

I've had my credit card stolen, and I can tell you, it's not a fun experience. It is a very arduous process to track down charges made by a stranger and have them reversed. My father had his brokerage account hacked as well, which was a very stressful experience. Fortunately he was able to get his money back, but many people aren't so lucky.

Identity theft and other breaches of cyber security are a relatively new form of invasive, criminal activity. A stolen identity can be devastating not only financially but emotionally as well. It is important to stay safe from this threat through care and vigilance.

Thieves can use even a little information to figure out a whole lot about you. Your date of birth, address, driver's license information, Social Security number, sex/gender, credit card numbers, and so on are all great boons to someone planning a cyber crime. How do they get this information? They can redirect your mail, steal data from a computer, steal your mail, steal your purse or wallet, or even go dumpster diving right outside your home. Unfortunately, some people will go to great lengths to make a living through dishonesty.

Take these pointers to heart, and keep yourself safe from identity theft and cyber attack:

- **Don't carry your essentials**. Unless it is specifically required at the time, don't carry essential documents with you like your Social Security card, birth certificate, or passport.
- **Shred**. It is a good idea to use a shredder to destroy any papers that may carry sensitive information before you discard them.

- **Be wary of phone callers**. Be careful when giving your info over the phone. Someone unscrupulous might easily pose as a telemarketer, a survey taker, or even a distant relative. Not giving out too much personal information over the phone may sound like common sense, but it is easy to forget some of these basic safeguards.

- **Limit downloads from websites you don't know**. This is an easy way to allow a virus or other tracking program into your computer, jeopardizing all your files and information, and possibly that of your friends. Be confident the site is authentic before you proceed.

- **Update your antivirus and spyware detection tools frequently**. Install a firewall to protect your home computer network. When you are not using your computer, turn it off.

- **Avoid banking by email**. You should never respond to email from what you think are financial institutions. Some phishing emails do a great job of mimicking the look and feel of companies you may trust. If you need to communicate with your financial institution, it is best to go directly to their website and use the secure login.

- **Take care when shopping online**. Purchasing items online potentially carries a similar risk. When shopping online, check on the authenticity of the website to make sure it is approved as secure, especially before divulging credit card information.

- **Destroy old electronic components when you are upgrading**. Destroy your hard drive when you are ready to get rid of an old computer. The same goes for your old cell phone. Don't discard either with data still on it, as it can be easily hacked.

- **Remember where you are**. If you are out and about and accessing a public Internet connection, don't send any sensitive information. Save your banking, shopping, and the like for a secure network you trust.

- **Limit information on social networking sites**. Don't be foolish and update your status with exactly how long you'll be leaving your house empty while you're on vacation. That's just a green light for a break in. Consider using nicknames only on those kinds of sites, and never post your phone number, address, or other essential information. When joining a social networking site, it is best to set your privacy preferences before you get started, and then proceed with discretion.

I have discussed a lot of rules and cautionary tales to help you maximize your ROI on safety. It really is a topic that crosses over to many aspects of life. In part that is the point. Living a safer life doesn't mean living in fear. Go out and live—drive, work, play, shop, and socialize. Do it all, but do it mindfully and healthfully. One oversight, mistake, or moment of poor judgment may not seem like a big deal at the time, but it can have huge ramifications for all your Core Assets. By reducing your risk in as many areas as possible, you increase your chances of what all of us hope to achieve: happiness, success, and a fantastically high ROI on life.

CAPS FOR YOUR ROI ON SAFETY 🔒

Use these **C**ORE **A**SSET **P**ROTECTION **S**TRATEGIES to keep safe.

1. **Don't let paranoia destroy you.** In other words, don't live in fear. If you have good safety awareness, remain well prepared, and are vigilant, you will be fine.

2. **Remember that insurance mitigates loss; it doesn't necessarily protect you from loss.** It can provide some degree of financial protection, but it will not reimburse you for time lost or the mental or physical anguish you may suffer from a bad event. Once again, don't fool yourself into thinking you are protected simply because you are insured.

3. **Shit happens no matter how well protected you think you are.** There's nothing you can do about it. Call it fate, karma, bad luck, whatever you like. Some things are simply out of your control. It is always best to focus on what you can control.

4. **Make the right choices.** These are common sense in nature. However, it is easier said than done. Prospectively a decision may seem safe, but retrospectively it may turn out to be a bad decision. As they say, don't cry over spilled milk. Instead, don't let it spill in the first place.

5. **Be prepared.** That's the famous Boy Scout motto I grew up with. Two simple words, yet two powerful, life-saving words indeed. No further explanation needed on this one.

6. **Stratify and prioritize your risks.** In other words, take into account the probability and severity of potential hazards and subsequent outcomes. For example, an elderly person has a higher probability of suffering a fracture from a fall than a young child does. The potential outcome is even more life-threatening for an elderly person than for a child. Therefore, taking measures to prevent elderly people from falling is of a higher priority than doing the same for a child.

4

Where You Live:
Your ROI on Physical Health

SETTING FOOT ON THE
PATH TO GOOD HEALTH

I admit it: I used to be a junk-food junkie. General carelessness was a hallmark of my diet plan. I'd eat whatever was the easiest thing to grab while on the go. Without forethought in the land of fast-food restaurants and convenience store snack aisles, we just aren't set up to make the healthiest choices.

Most of us enjoy an air of invincibility in our youth, and I was no exception. I honestly had no real concept of how bad my diet was. I thought I could eat anything—most of it nearly opposite to health professionals' advice—and I'd enjoy it without consequence. It was good while it lasted. As I got older, my metabolism slowed down and I gradually began to gain weight.

I noticed other changes as well. My joints started to have a touch of those aches I used to hear about in my grandparents' complaints. Around the same time, my cholesterol began measuring fairly high. I was relatively young when I began taking medication to lower it. Unfortunately, I was using the cholesterol medication as a crutch; I thought that if I just took the magic pill, I could continue to ingest anything I wanted.

After a year my body mass index had crept up higher than it should have been for my height and weight, and the medication I'd been taking was just not as effective. Finally I recognized that, along with the magic pill, I'd taken a big dose of plain old laziness. Add to that the side effects of muscle weakness and dizziness the medication seemed to be causing, and I knew I had to make a change. The effortless days of my youth had come to an end. It was time to start paying attention to the idea that a healthy diet and regular exercise are good for you. After all, I realized, my body is one thing I'll have all my life. Our bodies are where we live. I decided I'd better start taking good care of mine.

As funny as it is that it took a doctor so long to figure that out, I believe my personal journey gave me some good insight into how to help others get started on the path to good health. Recognizing that everybody is different, here are some basic tips on how to invest in your health for the very best ROI.

When you are ready to reach for optimum health, put first things first. Commitment is everything. Although it is wise to make gradual and enduring changes to your patterns of diet and exercise rather than drastic moves that won't be sustained, the initial step is simply to resolve to make those changes. Educate yourself about healthier foods. Find a good starting-point exercise program you can expand and modify as you go. Whatever you choose, acknowledge the shift that has taken place in your mind about health consciousness, and make the decision to stick to the program.

NUTRITION AND DIETING

It is no secret that a lot of us are obsessed with dieting. It seems also to be true that many health gurus, commercial enterprises, and the popular media are just as obsessed with bringing the next big diet to anyone who is ready to eat it up. With all the interest in dieting, why is obesity so prevalent that it has been recognized as a common chronic disease? Currently more than 50 percent of U.S. adults are classified as overweight or obese.

A significant problem with the typical Western diet these days is that once-reasonable levels of intake have shifted over time. Fat consumption, once 27 percent of the average diet, has managed to rise to 37 percent. The average adult in the United States used to consume 70 pounds of sugar a year. If that sounds like a lot, consider that sugar intake now tips the scale at 156 pounds per year according to the USDA (John Casey, "The hidden ingredient that can sabotage your diet" *MedicineNet.com*, Jan. 3, 2005).

In addition, the American Heart Association recommends no more than one teaspoon of salt daily, but for most of us that has moved closer to four teaspoons each day. Our overall daily calorie intake has gone up as well, while our consumption of nutrient-packed vegetables has gone down.

There are so many diets out there, it's simply a bit overwhelming. The Cookie Diet. The No Cookies Diet. Eat only meat. Go vegan.

Who is right? Do diets work? Do they have lasting power? Can the weight loss be maintained, or will you end up gaining it all back? Let's try to find some common ground.

REDUCING CALORIES FOR WEIGHT LOSS

No matter what diet you choose or plan to start, the bottom line remains caloric intake. Even if you consume the healthiest of diets and ingredients, so long as you take in more calories than you burn, you will not lose weight. Caloric balance is the key.

A good rule of thumb for healthy weight loss is to cut 500 calories a day to lose about 1 pound a week. If you cut 250 calories, count on losing half a pound a week. This process is accelerated when coupled with regular exercise. However, it is very difficult to count calories consistently. It can be done initially until your goals are reached. Once your new diet habits are established, you can wean yourself off of regular counting so long as you remain conscious of your consumption. For some people, even that may be extremely difficult. In that case, instead of counting, simply try to reduce your caloric intake when possible.

If you want to relive your old algebra classes, you can determine your daily caloric requirement by using a formula created by Drs. James Arthur Harris and Francis Gano Benedict—the Harris-Benedict Equation.

To avoid the pain of revisiting algebra, I have included Figure 4.1 to help you figure out where you stand with your BMI.

Height in Feet and Inches

Weight in Pounds	4'9"	4'11"	5'1"	5'3"	5'5"	5'7"	5'9"	5'11"	6'1"	6'3"
154	33	31	29	27	26	24	23	22	20	19
165	38	33	31	29	28	26	24	23	22	21
176	38	36	33	31	29	28	26	25	23	22
187	40	38	35	33	31	29	28	26	25	24
198	43	40	37	35	33	31	29	28	26	25
209	45	42	40	37	35	33	31	29	28	26
220	48	44	42	39	37	35	33	31	29	28
231	50	47	44	41	39	36	34	32	31	29
243	52	49	46	43	40	38	36	34	32	30
254	55	51	48	45	42	40	38	35	34	32
265	57	53	50	47	44	42	39	37	35	33
276	59	56	52	49	46	43	41	39	37	35
287	62	56	54	51	48	45	42	40	38	36
298	64	60	56	53	50	47	44	42	39	37
309	67	62	58	55	51	48	46	43	41	39
320	69	64	60	57	53	50	47	45	42	40
331	71	67	62	59	55	52	49	46	44	42
342	74	69	65	61	57	54	51	48	45	43
353	76	71	67	63	59	55	52	49	47	44
364	78	73	68	64	61	57	54	51	48	46
375	81	76	71	66	62	59	56	52	50	47
386	83	76	73	68	64	61	57	54	51	48
397	85	80	75	70	65	62	59	55	53	50
408	88	82	77	72	68	64	61	57	54	51
419	90	84	79	74	70	66	62	59	56	53
430	93	87	81	76	72	67	64	60	57	54
441	95	89	83	78	73	69	65	62	58	55
452	98	91	85	80	75	71	67	63	63	57

Healthy Weight
18.5–24.9

Overweight
25–29.9

Obesity
30– 4.9

Severe Obesity
35–39.9

Super Obesity
>40

Figure 4.1. BMI, Height, and Weight Chart

Tips and Tricks for Calorie Reduction

Even eliminating a small portion of daily calories without counting can go a long way. Here are a few tricks you can try to help reduce your daily caloric intake:

- Try using smaller plates and bowls as well as smaller serving and eating utensils.

- Start a meal with a salad and drink a glass of water before the meal to help reduce your appetite.

- Snack frequently, such as on small quantities of healthy nuts, to curb your appetite.

- Split or share a meal when you go out to eat; it not only saves calories but also your hard-earned money.

- Eat slowly. In other words, nibble and graze on your food. It takes twenty to thirty minutes for your brain to tell your body it's full.

- Order dressing on the side and minimize some of the tempting side dishes and condiments.

- Clean your pantry and cupboards of all the junk.

- Skip the dessert and the buffets. (These were one of my weaknesses—I used to be a kid in a candy store when I saw buffets. The all-you-can-eat cruises, all-inclusive trips, and Vegas buffets used to kill me. I would try to eat to get my money's worth.)

- Use some common reference points to help gauge your portions. For example, a clenched fist or baseball would amount to about one cup. A large egg or lightbulb would be about half a cup. The tip of your thumb would be one teaspoon. A poker chip would be about one tablespoon. A golf ball is about one ounce. You can go to choosemyplate .gov for more information on various portion sizes.

TIMING IS EVERYTHING WHEN EATING

As we discussed earlier, what and how much you eat are important, but *when* you eat can be just as critical. Starting your day off with breakfast seems like a cliché, but it's still very important. Loading up on calories early in the day not only provides much-needed fuel but also curbs your cravings. Unfortunately, it is usually the most-neglected meal of the day.

Protein should be a good part of your breakfast. Eggs, yogurt, soy milk, and nuts are all good examples of protein sources. Too many simple carbohydrates early on can invite a crash soon thereafter—not pleasant if you happen to be in an important meeting.

Oatmeal, a popular breakfast, is full of complex carbohydrates and fiber, which will not only provide needed fuel but will lower your cravings and help you feel full longer. Eating small meals and snacks throughout the day will reduce any sudden, intense cravings. Avoid eating late in the day. Try to eat dinner more than three hours before you go to bed so you aren't sleeping with a full stomach. Those excess calories don't get burned and eventually get stored as fat.

WHAT'S ON YOUR TABLE?

So what is on your table? First, it's important to eat a variety of foods that give you a good balance of carbohydrates, proteins, and healthy fats. From those healthy choices, find high-ROI foods that are especially rich in vitamins, minerals, and fiber. Here are some facts to help you choose foods that will give you a high ROI.

Choose Complex Carbohydrates

Some fad diets would have us believe we should avoid most or all carbohydrates, but the truth is they are vital for our health. Our bodies break down carbohydrates into simple sugars that serve as our main source of energy. Without carbohydrates, the primary cycle that produces energy for our bodies would cease to function.

The glycemic index for foods high in carbohydrates can help you distinguish healthier choices. Low glycemic–index foods break down slowly and don't cause blood sugar to rise so quickly. Try eating more low glycemic–index foods like apples, berries, cherries, barley, grapefruit, lentils, beans, peanuts and other legumes, almonds, walnuts, soy nuts, unsweetened oatmeal, green peas, tomatoes, and unsweetened yogurt. Low glycemic–index foods are slowly digested and absorbed. Therefore they produce gradual rises in blood sugar and insulin levels, not crazy spikes. They also improve both glucose and lipid levels in people with type 1 and type 2 diabetes. They help in weight control because they can also control appetite and delay hunger. Low glycemic-index foods reduce insulin levels and insulin resistance.

High glycemic–index foods contain refined carbohydrates that break down quickly, increase blood sugar rapidly, and cause spikes in insulin. Slow fat metabolism, low energy, and the dreaded sweet cravings are common responses to eating high glycemic–index foods. Your intake of high glycemic–index foods should be kept to a minimum. This includes candy, cookies, chips, white potatoes, most breakfast cereals, corn sugar (high-fructose corn syrup), sweetened soda, white bread, and bagels.

Glycemic loads are also helpful to know. They describe how many grams of food it takes to raise your glucose levels after eating. Even though loads are based on the glycemic index, some foods may have similar indices but different loads. Therefore the glycemic load provides complementary information on the impact of carbohydrate consumption.

Consume Good Fats

Also contrary to what you may have heard from fad diet advocates, some fats are necessary in a balanced diet. Fats are a concentrated source of energy. They help maintain the cell membranes and are important for the proper absorption of some essential vitamins. They are also important for the brain, which is composed of 60 percent fat.

Maintaining healthy fats in your diet can help maintain an essential component (myelin) of your nervous system. Myelin, which is composed of fat, can improve your cognitive function. The standard Western diet tends to rely too heavily on unhealthy fats, but concentrating only on eating no fat or low fat is not the answer. Moderate amounts of healthy fats are the way to go.

Healthy fats are found in lean meats, skinless poultry, and many fish. Monounsaturated and polyunsaturated fats are the ones to seek out. They help lower the LDL or "bad" cholesterol and total cholesterol levels, and reduce the risk of blood-clot formation. Some examples of monounsaturated fats are olive oil, canola oil, olives, peanuts, peanut butter, avocados, almonds, almond oil, and cashews. It is best if 30 to 40 percent of your recommended fat intake is made up of monounsaturated fats. A handful of raw nuts a day puts you well on your way to meeting your quota and gives you a shot of protein, too.

Polyunsaturated fats are found in safflower, soybean, sunflower, corn, cottonseed, and sesame oils. Eating a modest amount of natural foods that contain good fats is a better choice than buying low-fat, processed foods, which tend to be high in sugar.

Omega-3 fatty acids are also good for increasing HDL, or "good" cholesterol levels, lowering triglyceride levels, and helping to reduce the risk of heart attack. They are considered an essential brain food. Take fish oil; eat fish and other seafood; and have some leafy, green vegetables, tofu, nuts (especially walnuts and almonds), and flax seeds to increase your omega-3 intake. You can sprinkle ground flax seeds on yogurt, cereal, and salad, or use them as an ingredient in baked goods.

A great deal of research suggests there are benefits to including the right varieties of fish in the diet. The American Heart Association recommends two or three servings of fatty fish each week. Sardines, mackerel, salmon, tuna, trout, and herring fit the bill. The *New England Journal of Medicine* has said two fish dishes a week may cut the risk of dying of a heart attack by 50 percent.

Fine-tune Your Protein Intake

Amino acids in proteins are the building blocks of muscle tissue. Proteins are important for maintaining lean muscle mass, growth, and tissue repair. The making of hormones and enzymes depend on them, too.

Taking in enough protein is especially important because of the twenty amino acids, ten of which cannot be synthesized within the body. These essential amino acids must be consumed in foods or supplements.

Good sources of protein include lean meat and poultry, salmon, sardines, eggs, nuts, seeds, dairy products, peas, soy, black beans, and pinto beans. In the standard omnivorous Western diet, it is generally easy to get enough protein. The trick is to avoid taking in too much fat and cholesterol along the way.

It is best to eat limited portions of meat, eggs, and dairy. A clever way to do this is to remember to fill most of your plate with leafy greens and other vegetables. Adding animal protein to the plate last can keep your portion control in check. Vegetarians can seek out soy protein or an alternative.

Consider putting turkey on the menu even when it's not holiday season. Not only is it a good source of protein, but turkey also contains tryptophan, which increases mood-improving serotonin. This will help you resist cravings for simple carbs, keeping your overall diet in better balance.

Take Your Vitamins

This is important. Don't simply buy a bottle of the least-expensive drugstore supplements you can find. Isolated micronutrients don't do the job as well as whole foods do, so eating a variety of fresh vegetables to get the vitamins and minerals you need is the first place to start. Supplements made from whole, plant-based foods can provide a boost to fill in what an already healthy diet may be missing.

Try to get 400 milligrams of magnesium each day for heart rhythm and 600 milligrams of calcium twice a day for bone health, improved blood pressure, inflammation reduction, and more.

To absorb calcium, you need vitamin D (according to the USDA, 400 IU daily for those under the age of sixty; 600 IU for those over sixty). That means get out and enjoy the sun! Sunlight exposure for as little as fifteen minutes twice a week will often do the trick, although darker-skinned people may need more. Eggs, fatty fish, and vitamin D–fortified foods may help, but it is fine to supplement if you need to.

Vitamins C (600 milligrams twice daily) and E (400 IU daily) taken together make a powerful antioxidant combo.

Vitamins A, D, E, and K are fat soluble. That means they are best absorbed with fat-containing meals. Remember those good fats? Here is one of the ways they are very important. If you drink milk, low-fat, fortified milk may help get these vitamins into your system.

The B vitamins are also important. The folate (B9) found in foods is only partially absorbed, so a supplement is recommended. Add B6 and B12 for a more complete B spectrum intake. Overall, a good multivitamin that covers all these bases can keep your biological age more than six years younger than what the calendar tells you.

Remember the law of diminished returns? When it comes to vitamins, you *can* get too much of a good thing. You'll do well to avoid taking more than the recommended maximum of 2,500 IU of vitamin A daily. An overdose can lead to reduced bone mineral density, skin discoloration, hair loss, and even birth defects. Vitamin D is not typically recommended at daily doses higher than 600 IU. Its toxicity leads to calcium buildup in the blood, which facilitates problems including nausea and vomiting, weakness, constipation, heart arrhythmia, and kidney stones. The exception, of course, is if you are Vitamin D deficient. When taking supplements, always follow the directions.

Balance Your Electrolytes

Most of us really need to cut down on our sodium (salt) intake. But, at the same time, most of us also need to up our potassium to 4,700 milligrams a day. Potassium promotes healthy arteries, and you can get it by having four servings of fruit per day, especially bananas, avocados, and melon. Beans, fish, nuts, dark, leafy greens, and dairy products can also help keep your potassium balanced.

Add Fiber

Fiber is the nondigestible part of a plant, also known as *bulk*, *roughage*, and *bran*. The typical American diet has far too little fiber. It helps us feel full, and so it can help control weight. It can lower total and LDL cholesterol levels by interfering with its absorption in the digestive tract. Good fiber sources include oat bran, oatmeal, and barley; fruits like apples, oranges, strawberries, and prunes; and corn, broccoli, lentils, and navy beans. Psyllium husk, among a few other varieties, is available as a fiber supplement, but use it only in conjunction with balanced diet choices rather than as a sole source. As with anything else, all in good measure—too much fiber will interfere with the absorption of some much-needed vitamins.

Spice It Up

Many spices have natural qualities that aid in digestion and provide other benefits that are anecdotal. Capsaicin is one of the hottest spices. Chili peppers can vary from hot (jalapenos, pimentos) to extremely hot (habanera). They increase metabolism, reduce pain, guard against heart disease, reduce cluster headaches, may reduce blood pressure, help digestion, and can serve as a good appetite suppressor. Paprika also contains capsaicin. Cinnamon is known to help control blood sugar and is helpful to diabetics. It curbs sweet-tooth cravings. Ginger has anti-inflammatory properties and helps reduce motion sickness and nausea.

Garlic is an antiseptic considered to be helpful in lowering cholesterol and improving heart health. Turmeric is good for digestion, helps with asthma and colds, may delay the onset of Alzheimer's, and eases discomfort associated with the menstrual cycle. It acts as an anti-inflammatory agent and contains an anti-oxidant called *curcumin*. Oregano, thyme, and cumin are also known to be exceptional additives.

Get Your Flavonoids

These are powerful antioxidants that have overall anti-inflammatory effects on the body's systems. Thirty-one milligrams of flavonoids each day is recommended. You can take in the necessary amount by drinking two-and-a-half glasses of cranberry juice or several cups of tea. Also try nuts, grapes, red wine, 100 percent natural orange juice, onions, tomatoes, and tomato juice.

LOW-ROI FOODS AND INGREDIENTS

In contrast to our beneficial high-ROI foods, there are definitely foods to avoid at mealtime:

- **Refined carbohydrates are the enemy.** Simple sugars are simply no good for you, and please do your best to avoid **high-fructose corn syrup**. It is hidden in lots of products these days, sometimes labeled "corn sugar," and is a major culprit in the current epidemic of expanding waistlines. Just as diabetes can be brought on by overdosing on sugar that causes insulin spikes and eventual breakdown of the sugar regulation system, its effects can also be reversed by a diligent return to good food choices.

- **Keep saturated fats to a minimum.** Unlike the mono-unsaturated and some polyunsaturated fats that are useful to the body, saturated fats should be kept to a minimum. You'll find saturated fats in animal products like red meat, poultry skin, cheese, lard, and butter. A secondary source of saturated fats is tropical oils, mainly palm and coconut. Tropical oils in turn are often hidden ingredients found in processed foods like nondairy creamers, soups, potato chips, salad dressing, and crackers.

- **Trans fats are another no-no.** They are often found in margarines and shortenings, as they provide a nice texture and have a long shelf life. Don't fall for it. The American Heart Association recommends less than 1 percent of your calorie intake should come in the form of trans fats.

- **Lose the salt.** Salt is used prevalently in processed foods, which is yet another major reason to steer as clear of them as possible. Our tastes have become acclimated to high salt contents, so it is worth the effort to retune your taste buds by preparing foods at home with other flavorful herbs and spices while using less table salt, also known as sodium chloride. High sodium intake is linked to kidney and thyroid problems, stroke, and hypertension—a silent killer most common in the United States and Japan.

- **Avoid recreational beverages.** In the past twenty years, an enormous, billion-dollar industry has appeared in industrialized cultures around the world. These are the high-fat, sugary, afternoon coffee and fruit beverages sold at fast-food places. These beverages have a high profit margin for the restaurants but deliver huge doses of empty calories with zero nutrition. If you are eating a healthy diet, there is no reason to ingest 500 liquid calories in the middle of the afternoon. Switching to diet soft drinks may not be much better—recent studies suggest diet soda can actually increase your appetite. If you are thirsty, have some water.

More Bad Ingredients

Here is a handy list of foods and additives that are bound to give you a low ROI. Familiarize yourself with the items on this list so you know when to say "no" when you're in the grocery store looking at that ingredients list:

- Artificial colors (yellow #6, red #40, blue #1 or #2, green #3, etc.)
- Artificial sweeteners—aspartame (NutraSweet, Equal) and sucralose (Splenda®)
- Dextrose, sucrose, fructose
- Enriched, bleached wheat or white flour
- High-fructose corn syrup or corn sugar
- Hydrogenated oil or partially hydrogenated oil
- Monosodium glutamate (MSG)
- Natural and artificial flavors
- Palm oil

- Weird-sounding food chemicals (sodium benzoate, potassium bromate, acesulfame potassium, propyl gallate, butylated hydroxytolulene [BHT], butylated hydroxyanisole [BHA], sodium nitrate and nitrites)
- White processed sugar

REACH FOR HIGH-ROI FOODS

Certain tasty health enhancers have been shown to have such great benefits, they sometimes aren't referred to as mere foods. These are the **high-ROI foods**. Once you get the basics under control, consider incorporating some of these excellent dietary enhancers into your routine. If some of them are unfamiliar, it is well worth it to work on introducing them to your palate:

- **Berries**: These not only taste sweet, but they can also deliver sweet health results. Blueberries, blackberries, raspberries, and strawberries are high in phytonutrients that can prevent macular degeneration, heart disease, Alzheimer's, and high cholesterol; they even help fight cancer.

- **Cruciferous vegetables**: Broccoli, cabbage, bok choy, and cauliflower (and others) contain powerful anticancer phytochemicals and compounds that can help keep cancer away.

- **Onions, garlic, and ginger**: These can also be added to the cancer-fighting list. To seal the deal, a glass of broccoli juice has more calcium than a glass of milk.

- **Soy foods**: Tofu, soy milk, and edamame contain isoflavones that are also known to fight cancer. In addition they are good at supporting the immune system.

- **Macadamia nuts:** These may be relatively high in fats, but they contain heart-healthy oils that actually promote high metabolism and fat burning instead of fat storage.

- **Sprouts:** These are excellent sources of nutrition. Many beans and seeds can be sprouted easily in your kitchen, and alfalfa, mung bean, radish, and other sprouts are commercially available. They are loaded with vitamin C and digestive enzymes, and, most important, have the vital energy of a living food.

In addition to all the other goodness they have packed inside, nearly all high-ROI foods are very high in mood-stabilizing B vitamins. Sometimes feeling good is a first step to the consciousness required to take better care of your body. Do try to incorporate some of these wonderful health-enhancing foods into your life.

More Good Foods and Ingredients

Here is a handy list of foods, food components, and supplements that will give you an excellent ROI on nutrition. Make sure the fruits and veggies are raw and organic for the utmost nutritional impact:

- Avocados
- Barley grass
- Beans
- Beets
- Berries (blackberries, blueberries, raspberries)
- Broccoli
- Carrots, unpeeled
- Fish oil
- Flaxseed oil
- Garlic
- Ginger
- Lentils
- Macadamia nut oil

- Nuts (almonds, walnuts)
- Oatmeal
- Olive oil
- Pomegranate juice
- Radishes
- Seafood (salmon, tuna)
- Sea vegetables (kelp, kombu, nori, wakame)
- Soy products (edamame, tofu)
- Spinach
- Sprouts
- Tomatoes
- Wheat germ
- Wheat grass
- Yogurt (Greek)

More Food for Thought

Dark Chocolate

I'll admit I am a huge chocolate lover. This delicious favorite contains good-for-you antioxidants called *flavonoids*. Higher-end chocolate bars will generally list the amount of cocoa they contain. The higher the cocoa content, the more antioxidants present, and the greater the benefit.

Unfortunately, as the cocoa level goes up, the more bitter the taste becomes. It takes getting used to when you switch to dark chocolate. Cacao levels of 70 percent or greater are best. Be careful of additives such as sugar, cream, and butter. The not-so-great (albeit delicious) chocolates are white chocolate, milk chocolate, and hot cocoa.

Vinegar

Often used along with herbs and spices in salad dressings and other sauces, this fermented product is known to bring down blood sugar levels and is especially good when taken early in meals.

THE HIGH ROI OF WATER: A TRUE
FOUNTAIN OF YOUTH

The human body is made up of about 75 percent water and 25 percent solid material by volume. Brain tissue has an even higher water content of 85 percent.

To put this in perspective, consider an average man who weighs 175 pounds (79.37 kg). Of his total weight, 60 percent is water. That means that of the average 175-pound man, 105 pounds (47.62 kg) of him is nothing but plain water. The other 70 pounds are what we think of as being the person we know.

Obesity drives down the percentage of water to as low as 45 percent of body weight.

The water throughout our systems is one of the primary substances the body uses to regulate its functions. It is so important to our health that it deserves extra commentary.

A great deal can go awry without enough water. Dehydration can show up looking like many different health problems. For that reason it is significantly underdiagnosed. Some believe having a dry mouth is the only sign of dehydration, but in truth it is one of the late signs.

Symptoms of dehydration can include muscle cramps, heart palpitations, nausea, lightheadedness, weakness, and decreased or dark urine output.

The very best thing you can do to avoid any of these problems is to drink water, and plenty of it. The current recommendation states that people should drink six to eight glasses daily. But is this always the case? People come in all shapes and sizes, so I don't believe a blanket statement with a concrete amount is the best approach. It's best to drink water frequently before you notice the sensation of thirst. Drink it until you're naturally content so you have a regular urinary output. A pattern you might try is to have a glass of water automatically in the morning when you brush your teeth. Have a glass of water with each meal, one before exercising, and two after. Keep a pitcher or water bottle handy.

Keeping the body hydrated can do so many wonders. Water truly is the fountain of youth. It boosts your immune system and helps the body heal efficiently with tissue and DNA repair. It helps digestion by helping to break down and absorb food and its nutrients. It lubricates joints, eyes, and the mouth. It maintains normal spinal disc height for proper shock absorption, posture, and body support.

Good hydration also helps prevent strokes and heart attacks. Sweating helps regulate the body's temperature through both cooling and heating. It also helps get rid of bodily wastes such as urine and serves naturally as a stool softener. Moisture in the skin preserves your youthful complexion and glow.

Water provides an energy boost by preventing fatigue, especially during vigorous physical activity. Adequate hydration can boost your mood and concentration while preventing memory loss as you age. As mentioned before, it can be an effective appetite suppressor in weight loss. There are many more advantages to hydration—too many to mention.

The best kind of water to drink is still a highly debatable topic. If you obsess too much about the source of your water, you diminish the ROI by adding undue worry. Some people who become overly concerned with water purity choose distilled water, which has had minerals removed. We should all watch out for mineral deficiencies, so if you drink bottled water, choose one in which minerals are still present.

Plain old tap water might come to the rescue just as well. Some complain about "hard water," but it may not pose a problem at all for drinking. The dissolved calcium may actually be good for us. Tap water may also provide some of the iodine we need for the body's sodium-potassium pump to run smoothly, and to keep the thyroid healthy.

If you have concerns about high levels of chlorine in your tap water, the easiest remedy is to fill a jug and leave it open to the air. In half an hour, much of that chlorine will have dissipated. If the overall quality of your tap water concerns you, adding a solid carbon filter to the faucet can do the trick.

SURPRISINGLY BENEFICIAL BEVERAGES

Some foods just don't have the best reputations. However, there are benefits where you would not at first suspect. Take a look at this list and taste some vices that, in moderation, can actually be good for you.

Coffee and Tea

Many people automatically put all caffeinated beverages in the "bad" column, but this is worth reconsidering. Some coffee is actually pretty good for the heart. It can also be beneficial to type 2 diabetes, liver cirrhosis, dental cavities, Parkinson's disease, colon and prostate cancer, suicidal ideation, and asthma. It can also help with endurance and concentration, is known to treat headaches, and can reduce the risk of cardiac arrhythmia. A little caffeine can be good for reversing Alzheimer's disease and toning down ADD.

Green tea is another caffeinated beverage that is growing in popularity. It has some antioxidants, and the full range of its benefits is still being studied. However, coffee and other caffeinated beverages have a tight range of positive ROI. Too much caffeine can dehydrate the body, as you will begin to urinate out more fluids than you take in. Too much can also block melatonin, which regulates the sleep function, hence caffeine's trademark effect of wakefulness.

Alcohol

Most people are familiar with the cautionary tales—or bad jokes— about the effects of drinking one too many. However, an alcoholic beverage can be effective in reducing cardiovascular risk by increasing "good" cholesterol (HDL) and decreasing "bad" LDL. Alcoholic beverages, including beer, contain antioxidants that are sometimes more powerful than those in citrus fruits and black tea. Individuals who imbibe modest amounts of alcohol, notably red wine, have been found to have lower levels of C-reactive protein, a marker for inflammation.

But remember, this is definitely not a case where if a little is good, a lot must be better. It is easy to cross over into the zone of decreased ROI with dehydration, impotency, liver damage, immune system suppression, and other health and safety risks because of too much alcohol. Moderation is the key.

THE HERBAL PATH

Many doctors would have this to say about herbal remedies: don't even bother. They believe science has produced medicines superior to nature and you should always go for the prescription medication.

I happen to disagree. Mother Nature has given us some special plants that can be very helpful. Aspirin, for instance, comes from the active ingredient in willow bark (salicin), which is ultimately converted in the body into salicylic acid. Taxol, a cancer drug, comes from the Pacific yew tree. Morphine, a common painkiller, originates from an opium extract. Digitalis, a cardiac drug, comes from the foxglove plant family.

Herbal medicine has existed for centuries. More than 7,000 medical compounds in today's pharmacopeia are from plants. One hundred and twenty active ingredients have been isolated from plants that are used in modern medicine today. Germany is probably the most progressive when it comes to herbal medicine, with oversight from Commission E.

If you do take herbs to enhance your health, it is always best to buy them through good manufacturers that guarantee standardized doses. As always, consult your medical professional before embarking on any herbal therapy. Some herbs might be contraindicated for your condition or could conflict with medications you may already be taking.

That said, here is some helpful alternative-remedy information. You can buy herbals as liquids or solid extracts, tinctures, and powders, which are often sold in convenient capsules. It is generally better to purchase single-herb products than herbal formulas. Herbal teas are generally not that helpful. The herbs are often no longer fresh by the time you get them. If you do buy teas and bulk herbs, make sure they are still fragrant. That means there is less chance the active components have deteriorated.

BEST-KNOWN HERBALS

Here is a discussion of some of the best-known herbals. *Note*: Before adding any herbals to your daily routine, check with your doctor. This is especially important if you are taking prescription medications or if you have any mitigating medical conditions.

Aloe

The topical use of this plant increases blood flow to injured areas of the skin and promotes healing. It is an anti-inflammatory and a pain reliever. It is best to use in its purest form—straight from the live plant. Processing brings on substantial degradation of its positive effects.

Astragalus

A good enhancer of the immune system. It stimulates white blood cells, antibodies, and interferon. It may cause some bloating.

Echinacea

This popular herb is good for colds and flu. It has been officially approved in Germany for over-the-counter use for respiratory ailments. Like astragalus, it stimulates white blood cells and interferon. A tincture made from the root of the plant can be taken in water or tea four times a day. The German commission currently recommends this for no longer than eight weeks per treatment cycle.

Garlic

Not only does it taste good in tomato sauce and many other culinary endeavors, garlic has been said lower LDL cholesterol and to balance it with HDL cholesterol. Throwing an extra bulb of the stuff into your soup certainly can't hurt, but the simple addition of an OTC garlic tablet may prevent social concerns about garlic breath.

Ginkgo Biloba

This herb is helpful for improving brain function, memory, and concentration, and used to reverse vertigo. Ginkgo Biloba has also been proposed to treat Alzheimer's disease and other causes of dementia. The ideal dose is 120 milligrams daily in two to three separate doses (all dosing recommendations based on *Natural Standards;* ISBN 0-323-02993-0). Look for a label that says *24-6*, which means it contains 24 percent flavone glycoside and 6 percent turpenes. Ginkgo is well tolerated in most adults for up to six months, but there are risks of bleeding so it would not be advised for people on blood thinners or women who are pregnant or breast feeding.

Ginseng

This root of the plant genus Panax is known to be a stimulant and can be used to treat type 2 diabetes. Ginseng is also purported to be an aphrodisiac. You can find it as an extract in both liquid and solid forms; it is best to find one standardized to 4 percent ginsenoside. Possible side effects include insomnia, elevated or lowered blood pressure, nausea, diarrhea, and headaches. There are potential drug interactions, especially in people who are diabetic, because those individuals may tend to have lower blood sugar levels.

Green Tea

Also a good source of antioxidants. Black tea contains them as well, but less than its green counterpart. The plant sterols found in green tea help reduce the risk of heart disease. Again, when taking tea as an herbal supplement, only the freshest will do. Try to find a good source where the herb comes from harvest to you as quickly as possible.

Hawthorn

This is a derivative of a northern hemisphere shrub and is used to enhance heart health. It has similar properties to the cardiac medication called *digitalis*, which is derived from the foxglove plant. Hawthorn helps prevent oxidation of LDL cholesterol. If you have heart failure, it is imperative to use it only under a doctor's supervision.

Kava

Kava has been called a natural Valium. It is more appealing to many than "mother's little helper" because it calms the nerves without narcotic or strongly addictive effects. Still, long-term use should be avoided. Taking a capsule standardized to seventy to eighty-five kava lactones may be useful for treating anxiety. Taken just before bedtime, it can relieve insomnia.

St. John's Wort

Contrary to my first thought when I first heard of it, it is neither made from, nor will it give you, warts. In fact it is used to elevate mood and alleviate mild depression. Its effects take some time—a 3 percent hypericin extract should be used daily for up to six weeks in order to begin to see results. In some cases it may cause photosensitivity. Use of this supplement should be closely monitored by a trained medical professional because there can be interactions with some prescription drugs and other supplements.

Saw Palmetto

This one is good for the men. The oil-based extract of saw palmetto works to improve benign prostatic hyperplasia, or enlargement of the prostate. With the use of this herb, improvement may be seen in four to six weeks. Upset stomach has occasionally been reported as a side effect.

Valerian

This is another sleep aid in the herbal arsenal. One teaspoon of the tincture in one to two ounces of water usually helps bring on sleep within half an hour. One extra benefit is that this herb does not suppress the important nightly cycles of REM sleep. It is not good to combine valerian with other sedatives.

MORE SUPPLEMENTS TO CONSIDER

Coenzyme Q10

Also called *ubiquinone*, this alternative supplement is a powerful antioxidant. The Japanese government has approved it to treat congestive heart failure. It is also helpful in treating Parkinson's disease. The optimal dose is 1,200 milligrams daily. A doctor's advice is always paramount when dealing with heart health concerns. This supplement is sometimes used as an adjunct to cholesterol-lowering statins in order to prevent side effects such as muscle weakness.

Digestive Enzymes (Probiotics)

The gastrointestinal tract is full of microorganisms, with more than four hundred different bacterial species. While a few are located in the stomach and small intestine, most reside in the colon. These little critters actually do us a lot more good than harm. They help digest food, absorb nutrients, and enhance our immunity.

Sometimes the delicate balance can get out of whack, especially if we are stressed out, maintain a poor diet, or were recently on

medications such as antibiotics. Probiotics contain bacteria and/
or yeast, which can restore balance. Different kinds of probiotics
include microorganisms such as lactobacillus, streptococcus ther-
mophilus, and bifid bacteria, to name a few.

Now you've got quite a shopping list for outstanding nutrition,
and some additional pointers on herbal supplements that can help
you along the way. Let's move on to how to get your very best ROI
on another big component of physical health: exercise.

EXERCISE: MOVE YOUR BODY

After air, water, food, and shelter, the next most important thing for
survival is exercise. Despite living in the age of hundreds of cable television channels and one-click online shopping, we humans are simply
meant to be physically active. Even if you've been a couch potato up
to this point, it's never too late to get up and get into the exercise
groove. Any day—today, in fact—is the perfect time to start.

Like most of the good-for-you things to do for your body, there
is a long list of the benefits to exercise. Moving your body does
more than help keep you slim and beautiful, it stimulates the fat-
burning mechanism and raises the overall metabolism, which are
effective avenues toward losing weight. Exercise helps strengthen
the bones, which prevents osteoporosis. Working up a sweat assists
in the production of enzymes you need to convert stored energy
into useful energy. It builds muscle mass and generates a positive
nitrogen balance, preventing muscles from being used up as the
body's fuel. Getting in motion activates the sympathetic nervous
system and causes the secretion of histamine, which can prevent
asthma and allergic reactions.

Even if you aren't convinced for other reasons, consider the pursuit of pleasure. Staying in shape helps improve libido and heighten

sexual performance. Exercise also stimulates the production of endorphins, the natural opiate of the body. If there's a better sex life and a healthy, natural high to be had, why not go for it?

GETTING MOTIVATED

For some of you, I'll bet exercise sounds like a terrible chore. It would mean taking time away from your TV show or video game to do what? Run in place on a treadmill or ride a bike that never gets you anywhere? Don't worry—exercise doesn't have to be that boring. Remember when you were a kid and you loved running around and doing things outside? Well, you still can.

It's true. You don't necessarily have to go to a gym, although there are plenty of good ways to work out in that setting. Even if you are a gym rat, there are great benefits to getting out in the open air and enjoying being active. Your exercise can be done in whatever ways strike your fancy. Try walking, running, skiing, or playing tennis. Do you enjoy cycling around town or going out dancing? Those are great ways to exercise, too. With a little planning you can make your active time a natural part of your leisure activities.

I have to admit, my affinity for exercise has been much more of a journey than a constant oasis of perfection. When I was in college, I was into it. I loved sports like basketball, tennis, and flag football, and I was definitely into hitting the weight room. Unfortunately I didn't have the best technique, and aside from the occasional workout buddy who'd spot me on the weights, I had little guidance. My efforts and lack of know-how landed me with a hernia. Consequently the heavy weightlifting had to go, but I did try keeping up by adding a little more aerobic training.

Well, as things go, I started to let the aerobic workout slip as well. Getting older slowed down my metabolism, and before I knew it I had a bit of a problem with weight and cholesterol. I tried taking a pill to bring the bad cholesterol number down but wasn't yet ready to make a lifestyle change.

Like everybody else I had to live and learn. Even if I didn't think I had the time, it was time to *make* time. I got more into aerobic training. I added some calisthenics and some core exercises. It's been a few years now, and I'm still at it. Exercise has gone a long way toward getting my weight and cholesterol numbers to where they should be, and lo and behold, I feel a whole lot better.

The standard recommendation for frequency of exercise is three times a week. Given the modern, sedentary lifestyle, that's probably not enough. Since so many of us don't move a great deal in our daily lives except from the couch to the car to the office chair, some form of purposeful movement or exercise should be done daily. The gym is great, but starting out easy by walking in town or doing something at home can benefit you greatly.

Hopefully you will be able to have some fun and games along the way, but getting enough exercise does depend on another factor: commitment. There is the physical commitment of actually doing the activities. But there's also the mental commitment—the decision that must come before the action. It is easy to make excuses, so you've got to put getting enough exercise high on your priority list. The circumstances people need to stick with a program vary, but some suggest mentally putting the desired behavior in line with things you do every day without question. If making the time to exercise has historically been a struggle for you, try treating it the same way you treat brushing your teeth or nourishing your body. It will soon become a natural part of living. Just as you engage in conditioning the body, you will be conditioning the brain and orienting it toward better health. Mind over matter, as they say, really can do the trick.

Ready to go? Just put your mind to it. Snag yourself an exercise buddy, if you like, for moral support. Then shout a resounding, "YES!"

But wait—you say you usually aren't in an optimal place to exercise? You can find a way. At your work desk, you can flex your muscles and do some stretching on regular intervals or as needed. The simple act of choosing the stairs over the elevator in your building can add up to positive momentum. You can find a way to move your body at just about any time.

Congratulations! You're really all out of excuses now.

EXERCISE SAFETY

When you are starting out on any new exercise practices, safety is very important. It is wise to hire a personal trainer or an expert in your favorite sports activity. You'll need to learn to use the proper form. While it is imperative to get the body moving, moving in the wrong way, especially repeatedly, can cause damage. Someone familiar with your chosen exercise program will be able to give you tips on everything from warm-up and cool-down periods, lifting the proper amount to begin weight training, holding your posture in alignment in yoga class, or breathing healthfully and strategically while going for another lap in the pool. It is often the things that are easiest to forget—like proper posture and breathing—that hold incredible value for your safety and progress.

EXERCISE TYPES

There are three main types of exercise. It is important for all of us to do something from each exercise category on a regular basis:

- **Aerobic activities**, like tennis or jogging, are heart healthy and build endurance.

- **Anaerobic activities** include weight training and other muscle-building workouts.

- **Flexibility exercises** keep your body supple and able to perform its full range of motion with ease.

Aerobic

Walking is one of the simplest and most effective exercises. For most of us, taking a walk can be very enjoyable. Rev it up to a brisk pace, and you've got an aerobic exercise that is fun, too. It's nice to take a leisurely stroll anytime, but keep in mind that building up to a higher intensity makes the excursion heart friendly. In fact the faster the speed of your aerobic activity, the more you work the cardiovascular system. Lower intensity over a longer period of time tends to burn more fat.

The positive side effects of aerobic exercise include improved brain health, as increased circulation to the brain increases attentiveness and stimulates brain tissue growth. A brisk walk or another aerobic exercise of your choice is also a good way to keep the endorphins flowing. If you happen to be under stress, as so many of us are, aerobic exercise can come to the rescue. See if you can notice a mood elevation after something as simple as a walk downtown.

Anaerobic

Taking part in anaerobic exercise (weight lifting, strength training, etc.) will indeed help you make progress toward sculpting a beautiful body. Some of you may start out because you want to achieve upper-body definition or nice abs. Even if you come to it from a vanity perspective, you can expect to attain greater strength and improve your body mass index (BMI) as a result. Add to that the help it gives with avoiding or decreasing the effects of type 2 diabetes and arthritis. After your push-ups, leg presses, or bicep curls, the body continues to burn energy while healing the muscles that were exercised. That's one of the truly great things about anaerobic exercise—this type of muscle building burns fat even when you're just sitting around.

Flexibility

Flexibility and stretching exercises are wonderful on their own, but they are very important in conjunction with other activities. Try stretching after a workout while your muscles are still warm. You will reduce muscle soreness while avoiding injury from stretching cold muscles. Work with all the major muscles you used during the workout, holding each stretch for fifteen to thirty seconds. Give some extra attention to areas that seem particularly tight. Allow yourself to feel gentle resistance without causing pain or overextension.

Other benefits of stretching include getting more blood and nutrients to the tissues, improving coordination and posture, and reducing lower back pain. Any time of day, for a little me-time break, or after an intense workout, stretching can feel very good, like a reward for work well done.

FITNESS TRENDS

So where would you like to begin? Because the possibilities for exercise are so varied, you won't really find an exhaustive list of activities to try. Here instead is an overview of exercises that, when done properly and consistently, will give you a high ROI for your time and effort.

Aerobic Training

A few good aerobic exercises are walking, climbing stairs, cross-country skiing, step aerobics, rowing, and swimming. These examples are considered low-impact. High-impact aerobic exercises include dancing and dancercise, tennis, racquetball, and running. Most healthy adults should choose among low- and moderate-impact aerobic exercises. Higher-impact workouts may not be for those who are out of shape, have injuries, are older, or have proscriptive medical conditions. If you have any doubt, contact a medical professional.

A thirty-minute, low-impact workout is often a good place to start, with sixty minutes of combined lower- and higher-impact exercises as a goal to strive for as your endurance increases. It is recommended that you aim for an intensity that gets the heart pumping and works up a sweat, while still leaving you with the ability to have a conversation. If you are huffing and puffing, dial it back a bit. You will be able to do more in time, and your talking pace will increase naturally. Three to four hours per week of aerobic exercise is very good, but a daily or near-daily cardio workout will do wonders. Interval training, in which you alternate from low- to high-impact aerobic activity, has also been shown to be quite effective.

Running and Jogging

Among aerobic exercises, these are particularly popular. You really only need a pair of good running shoes and your enthusiasm. You can begin your program by walking briskly a few times a week. Eventually you will be able to transition into a walking/jogging combo, then all jogging, and so on until you are able to run the distance you desire. Running and jogging three to four times a week is sufficient; take days off or intersperse low-impact exercise to give the body a rest.

Most people benefit from running shoes that balance cushioning and motion control. Your sports equipment specialist and/or medical professional can give you the best advice to help you find the running shoes for your foot structure. Because running and jogging are among the most-high-impact aerobic exercises, injuries can be an issue. This makes the need for medical advice and proper shoes all the more important.

Once you heed the cautions and take up the sport, benefits abound. Running and jogging reduce the risk of heart disease, osteoporosis, diabetes, obesity, and even some cancers. Cholesterol and blood pressure may both be lowered. Other bonus benefits include lower anxiety and a decrease in reports of depression.

Cycling

A simple and very enjoyable way to get some exercise into a busy schedule, cycling is especially healthy because it gets the blood pumping and works the muscles, so it provides both aerobic and anaerobic benefits. Not only does it increase muscle tone in the legs and buttocks, but it also helps bring about more mobility in the hips and knees. Since cycling is a whole-body activity, it improves overall coordination. The bike definitely gives a boost to heart health and overall stamina. Cycling is a great calorie burner at 30 calories per hour. Thirty minutes a day of cycling for a year will burn away 11 pounds of fat.

One of the many great things about cycling is that you can do it almost anywhere. During inclement weather or any day you prefer the gym, you can always take a spin on a stationary cycle. On other days all you need is a bike and a proper street or trail. If you live in a place that is conducive, consider riding your bike to work or around town on errands day.

Always be safe and wear a helmet. Consider cycling an activity that can be done for life. Riding a bike is something you never forget how to do.

Water Exercise

Swimming is excellent exercise. Even if you aren't ready for a program of intense laps in an Olympic-sized pool, movement through water can be great for overall toning of the body. Water jogging, water polo, and gentle water aerobics are good examples of other exercises you can try.

A water workout is good for people of varying ages and abilities, and a main feature is that less pressure is placed on the back and the joints than with running. Its benefits include lowering blood pressure and cholesterol, loss of body fat, and raising overall energy levels, and it's an ideal exercise for those with arthritis. Some people who deal with chronic pain find that being in water relieves it to some degree, making exercise more manageable and enjoyable.

Strength Training

Strength or resistance training does triple duty by building muscle, burning fat, and maintaining bone density all at the same time. It is achieved by working various muscle groups with intense activity for a short time period. For example, a typical protocol during a workout would be to lift two dumbbells eight to fifteen times with two repetitions each, with a rest in between each set of repetitions. Free-weight lifting, pull-ups, tricep curls, and incline bench presses are just a few of the exercises among a vast array available in strength training.

How much should you try to lift? One rule of thumb is to use the weight that is half of what would make you exert the maximum effort for only one repetition. So if it takes all your effort to do one curl with a 30-pound weight, you may want to try starting your reps with a 15-pound weight.

Both muscle-shortening and muscle-lengthening exercises are important. Shortening happens during the up motion when lifting a weight, while lengthening comes about with the down motion. Increased awareness of the importance of the down motion has led to recommendations for lowering weights with slower, more controlled motions. A complete strength training session will typically begin by working with large muscles at high intensity and end with smaller muscles at lower intensities. Using proper form to isolate the correct muscle groups while not causing injury is essential. Breathing during strength training should also be intentional, with the out breath as the motion begins and the in breath as the motion returns to the beginning position.

Kettle Bell

Just in case you were wondering, the kettle bell has nothing to do with kettle corn or making tea. Also called a *girya*, it is a kind of cast-iron weight. Workouts with the kettle bell fit easily into the strength-training category, although its unique design also gives cardiovascular and some flexibility benefits at the same time.

The kettle bell looks something like a cannonball with a handle; its center of mass does not fall in the center of the hand like a dumbbell, but beyond it. Exercise moves done with this piece of equipment get the whole body involved and are called names like the *clean and jerk*, the *swing*, and the *snatch*. It is a good idea to be sure you have strong core muscles and a healthy back and shoulders before taking on the kettle bell.

Plyometrics

Athletes training to take it to the next level of speed and strength often practice these moves. Plyometric training is characterized by big, bounding movements like jumping, which require intense muscle contractions in quick succession. Specific exercises are often chosen to help a person improve his or her game, whether it's running faster, hitting harder, or nailing more slam dunks. You don't have to be a bona fide athlete to do plyometrics, but it would be a good idea to work hard at strength, balance, and agility, and to develop core strength before taking it on under supervision. It has been suggested that you should be able to do five squats with 60 percent of your body weight before graduating to plyometrics.

Isometric Exercises

Categorized with resistance training, the difference is that the muscles do not change length during the exercise. Instead they are made to exert a force against an immovable object, such as pushing against a wall, or a weight is held in a single position for a given duration. Because the muscles contract and are held in one specific position, similar holds at other angles are necessary to build or maintain strength across the range of motion.

This type of exercise is used most frequently in physical therapy or rehabilitation. The static nature of isometric exercises means many of them can be done with little or no special equipment. This can be a benefit over its dynamic strength-training counterpart. Participants should be aware that long isometric holds could raise blood pressure, so proper caution and awareness of health issues are advised.

Core Exercises

These work the muscles around the trunk and pelvis. They focus on the deep abdominal muscles that are not fully reached by basic sit-ups. Having a strong core improves balance and stability, strengthens the lower back, and makes all everyday or athletic activities easier to perform. Unfortunately, core exercises are too often neglected in workout routines.

Here is an alternate abdominal crunch that works the core: Lie on your back and place your feet on the wall in front of you. With hips and knees bent at ninety degrees, raise your head and shoulders. Performing sit-ups with the lower back supported by an exercise ball is another variation. With repetition, the tightening of the abdominal muscles will get results. If you enjoy the elliptical cross trainer machine at the gym, try pedaling without holding on. At first it will be difficult, but in time, you will be able to do it through an increase in core strength. Any exercise that gives you the opportunity to use the muscles of the trunk to maintain balance gives your core a workout.

Pilates

This type of exercise, now popular in many workout centers and sometimes blended into yoga classes, is most often done on a mat as a series of floor exercises. Named after Joseph Pilates, a German physical culturist in the late 1800s, Pilates focuses on the core muscles and emphasizes body position and control of movements. Through this method you can build up your core strength while generating energy and gaining power in the other major muscle groups as well. Pilates works to address the problem found with some exercises, like weightlifting, in which specific muscle groups can be worked to the hilt, causing short, tight muscles, while others are virtually ignored.

The hundred is a classic Pilates mat exercise. While lying on your back you work to pull in the belly button toward the lower back to engage the abdominals. Your head and shoulders should be lifted, and the legs are lifted several inches off the ground with toes pointed. While the abs are fully at work in this position, perform five quick in-breaths and five quick out-breaths while your arms are straight at your sides, performing controlled pumping motions. Repeat for a cycle of ten full breaths. A qualified Pilates instructor can provide exact body position and modifications.

Swiss Ball

A useful tool seen in most gyms today, it's known by many names including *exercise ball, stability ball, body ball,* and *yoga ball.* Working with it improves balance, core strength, and coordination. Excellent characteristics of the Swiss ball include its low cost, versatility, and portability.

Lying on your back, you can use the strength in your abs to pass the ball with your feet to your hands, lengthen the body fully, and then pass the ball with your hands to your feet, and continue the cycle. Back bends performed with the Swiss ball help stabilize and strengthen the back. Because of its inherent instability, using the ball like a bench while using free weights adds extra value to an upper-body workout by working the core. Stretching exercises done on the Swiss ball facilitate flexibility and can help with finding the perfect stretch or pose for deep relaxation.

Tai Chi

This is a martial art that uses slow, circular movements and a unique breath pattern meant to maximize the flow of what Eastern-influenced philosophy calls the *life force energy*, or *chi*. Tai chi has actually undergone a great deal of allopathic medical research, and its therapeutic value is well documented. Its breathing exercises have the ability to improve breathing capacity and reduce stress. The various exercises performed give the body the opportunity to move through wide ranges of motion, which is always a good way to keep the joints supple and muscles engaged. Especially helpful for older people and those who may be restricted from other exercise activities, tai chi can be of benefit to the bodies and minds of people of all ages.

Yoga

When I used to think of yoga, what came to mind were images of Indian gurus twisted into various pretzel shapes, wearing their traditional orange garb. While there was and still is Vinyasa, Hatha, and other traditional forms, now it has gotten so mainstream in the Western world that there are many new variations like surfboard yoga, disco yoga, and tantra yoga, just to name a few.

The word *yoga* is Sanskrit for *union*. In its essence its focus is on unifying body, mind, and spirit, and human with divine essence. Whether you follow yogic philosophy, much can be gained by adding the practice to your routine. Most yoga studios focus on *asana*, which involves taking on various seated, standing, or lying down postures while paying close attention to form and breathing. I love the new creative names given to the traditional yoga poses and movements. I don't think it is meant to be disrespectful at all. The Sanskrit names are simply too hard to pronounce, let alone remember. I would have liked the *bend over Rover* position, but thankfully downward dog is commonly used. Other poses include the chair, tree, fish, and mountain; all emphasize development of flexibility, balance, and specific positioning while paying attention to the breath and encouraging a relaxed attitude.

Yoga comes in many forms, from gentle Hatha and Yin varieties to the spiritually focused Anusara, to the more physically demanding Bikram and Ashtanga. The benefits of yoga are many. Some examples of the high ROI on this ancient and evolving practice include stress and anxiety reduction, pain relief (especially for weak backs), breathing improvements (good for asthmatics), flexibility, and a lowering of blood pressure and heart rate.

CAPS FOR ROI ON PHYSICAL HEALTH

These **C**ORE **A**SSET **P**ROTECTION **S**TRATEGIES are a few extra tips for reaching the heights of your physical well-being.

1. **Make dietary and exercise changes slowly.** If it has taken you all your life to get out of shape, it's okay if it takes a little while for you to move into better health patterns. Changing everything about your diet overnight might only succeed in making you resentful. Too much sudden exercise after a long career of watching television will hurt so badly you'll never stick with it. Be diligent and determined about making changes, but don't do too much too fast. You will be surprised by how a series of small changes eventually add up.

2. **Culture counts.** When working to improve your diet, be sure to allow for the cultural and ethnic foods that make you happy. Some familiarity and favorites in conjunction with important dietary shifts will yield results rather than make you feel dreary. Missing red sauce as an Italian or feeling horrible about taking fish oil if you are a longtime vegetarian doesn't have to be part of the plan. You can cut down or modify recipes and make substitutions, but don't cut out your family traditions entirely or go against your core beliefs. The idea is to feel good. Find ways to let your favorite foods in on the journey.

3. **Have another drink (of water, that is).** I know I mentioned water quite a bit in this chapter. Believe it or not, there is still more. You have probably heard that you should drink a lot of fluids when you're sick. This is true. When you're congested, drinking extra water can clear up your sinuses. When you are working on losing some weight, consuming water helps keep

you feeling satisfied so you feel less desire for unnecessary snacking. Remember to drink up!

4. **Don't forget to breathe.** This one sounds like a no-brainer. If you forget to breathe for too long, you won't be reading this. However, when you exercise there's more to breathing; you need to do it right. Never hold your breath while lifting weights, which could cause dizziness, nausea, hernia, heart attack, and other bad results. A good rule of thumb is to exhale on the exertion, taking one full out and in breath for each rep. For runners, they say a three-to-two inhale-to-exhale ratio is ideal to give you enough oxygen. Concentrate on filling your lungs, perhaps for longer than is usual, and you will develop good breathing habits to stay safe and optimize exercise time.

5. **Calculate your target heart rate.** It is a good idea to get to know your heart rate. Your resting heart rate is usually somewhere between sixty and eighty beats per minute. Your maximum is usually said to be 220 minus your current age. Your target heart rate—the number you should aim to maintain for the majority of your workout—is 50 to 75 percent of your maximum heart rate. Have a trainer observe your workout and help you determine your personal optimal heart rate for best results.

6. **Keep at it, but change it up.** Muscle memory is a phenomenon that happens once you've done an exercise for some time and your body eventually learns just what to do. This is what gives someone a great backhand, throw, or golf swing. But doing the same exercise and only that exercise causes the body to plateau, and you'll start to notice the workout

feels too easy and you're not progressing. Change your routine periodically to introduce some muscle confusion. That just means different muscle groups are given new tasks. So keep working at your favorite sport or fitness activity to get better and better at it, but throw in some other fun moves. You'll get fit, you won't get bored, and your muscles will kick it back into high gear.

5

Affairs of the Mind:
Your ROI on Intellectual,
Emotional, and Mental Health

EDUCATE TO LIBERATE

You may think that as a doctor, I would mainly sing the praises of formal education. True, I am fortunate to have received a good higher education that yielded positive benefits for my life today. I highly recommend it.

However, when I look back and wonder what I'd go back and change if I could, I don't wish that I'd taken a tougher Introduction to Biochemistry for some greater foundation in my work. In fact, I would have done well to have learned something about cooking. Most of us of a certain age remember being offered a class in high school called Home Economics, or Home Ec for short. Like me, you may have thought it was the equivalent of basket weaving—just a fluff course you didn't need, or a class for girls that would be embarrassing for a guy to take. In retrospect I can see that Home Ec generally teaches a lot of the things I might have been better off knowing about when I started life out on my own.

Whether your primary interest is computer programming, food preservation, aerospace engineering (yes, rocket science), political science, or anything else that strikes your fancy, one of the very best things you can do for yourself is get an education. This may sound like a tired old saying, but "knowledge is power" really couldn't be truer. Education comes in several major categories, and far be it for me to say that learning to be a whiz at calculus trumps learning how to fix your sink. Various societies tend to value some kinds of knowledge over others, but the truth is that no matter what direction you choose, learning throughout life is the key. Just as in the last chapter we concentrated on exercising your body, reaching for a great ROI on intellectual and mental health means making sure you keep your brain in good shape.

Since regular book learning is what we generally think of when we mention education, let's begin there. Here is a brief overview of the categories we tend to talk about when discussing education.

FORMAL EDUCATION

It's all about academics. What are the laws of physics that govern our world? Who were the most influential historical figures in your country in the nineteenth century? How do you draw a graph that can describe the current economic trends? What are the main differences between the poetry of the Moderns versus the Beats? These are the kinds of questions answered by the subjects we study in our primary school systems. Students are not only gathering a wealth of information about civics, science, math, language, and history; they are also gaining experience in how to function well with others in society.

One of the useful things about a formal education is that it gives young people a common baseline of understanding that grows as they grow. It is something the majority of us grow up with. Preschool and kindergarten get us used to social situations and how to behave in a classroom setting. We move on in elementary school to more complex social situations and stronger ties with friends. High school, college, and beyond deepen the well of knowledge and information while providing us good chances to develop responsibility and critical thinking.

The ROI on formal education really can't be overemphasized. It is linked with better health, a longer lifespan, improved self-confidence, higher self-esteem, and higher income potential. Getting a good education can't guarantee more success in life; unfortunately, nothing can do that. But would you like to increase your probability of success significantly? Taking your education seriously will give you a huge boost. If you are a parent or an otherwise significant influence in the lives of young people, helping them make the decision to stay in school and go on to college will be a great gift.

Just when you thought I'd given enough praise to formal education, there's more. Did you know that by getting a formal education, you not only better your odds of career success, but you are likely to wind up with more time for leisure and social activities? You have a better chance of being relaxed and more creative. With a good job and ample free time, artistic expression and entrepreneurial spirit have better chances to shine.

An overall educated society is considered a safer society, usually with less violent crime. Education is associated with a lower risk of incarceration, lower unemployment and poverty, and less need for social safety programs. The higher earning potential that comes with education leads to higher tax revenues and helps improve the standard of living. That's great news; not only do individuals benefit from the high ROI on formal education, but the community is better for it, too.

CONTINUING EDUCATION

It's good to know that education doesn't have to stop at the end of high school, job training, or college, or even with a post-graduate degree. If you are a chemist, you can continue taking courses to keep up with the latest body of knowledge. If you are a massage therapist who specializes in Swedish and deep tissue massage, learning Thai massage could be a great addition to your repertoire. You may have dual degrees in biochemistry and communications and work as a medical journal editor, but you still might want to go to night school for a course in something you've always loved, like photography. No matter the reason, there is no limit to what you can choose to study. Whenever you do, it is good for the mind and often the spirit, so it is time well invested.

Continuing education, like the formal education that has come before it, has the power to lead to a positive ROI for careers. It helps improve your chances of higher income. It can contribute significantly to improving your job skills so you don't become obsolete. Think of continuing education as a form of career insurance: when unexpected changes in the job market come around, you'll be in a much better position if you've been learning all along. The fact that you are prepared for future changes in your field is good for everyone in our ever-evolving society.

The good that continuing education can do for you personally might well be immeasurable. By enrolling in new classes, you will meet new people, and one of them could be your next big business contact or your new best friend. Just by being out and about in a thinking, learning environment, life tends to improve. Remember: opportunities abound!

LIFE SKILLS AND VOCATIONAL EDUCATION

This is the category where Home Ec and similar courses belong. Life skills that can be taught in the classroom as well as at home include cleanliness, hygiene, nutrition, and cooking. These are bits of knowledge that can raise the ROI not only on education, but also on health for individuals and families. How to deal with laundering and ironing your clothing are valuable skills as well. So are interior design and home furnishing. Contrary to what popular media might have you believe, those abilities are not strictly for people enacting shock-value home makeovers on reality TV.

When I was first living on my own, I could manage to screw in a lightbulb, but I didn't know much else in the realm of handyman activities or the daily caretaking of a home. I figured out quickly that knowing how to roll up my sleeves and wield a hammer or a plunger would be more helpful around the house than the information I'd mastered in Calculus II. Don't get me wrong—calculus is important in some professions and can serve as a brain-strengthening course for anyone who takes it. However, I do believe I would have had a head start on independent living if my background had included more day-to-day home activities.

I believe it should be mandatory for all students to take at least one life skills course. I managed to figure it all out as most of us do, but I would have been more ready to take on the dorms, my apartments, and finally my own house with this kind of knowledge at the ready. What a time-saver and a jumpstart all students would have if their background in life skills were already in place.

Physical education classes definitely fall under the category of life skills. In school I had some physical education classes that were fun, and I learned fencing and played soccer. There were some other enjoyable classes, and getting exercise is always good, but most of what we did in those courses didn't have a lifelong carryover. The ROI on education goes down when what is being taught doesn't stick. It would be a great shift if schools offered classes on yoga, Pilates, and good weight training form—all activities that can be more easily sustained for ongoing good health.

Vocational education prepares students for particular trades and job skills. These might include mechanics, carpentry, electrical work, Information Technology, or plumbing. Just as being functional in Home Ec is of benefit to students and their loved ones, gaining some basic knowledge in any number of trades is always a positive. For some people it will lead to the discovery of a talent and a lasting vocation. For others, a little more knowledge when discussing exhaust system repair with their mechanic certainly can't hurt. I am very grateful for what I've learned on the fly around the house. I hope that vocational and life skills education will someday take their rightful places of respect alongside the formal education achievements that our culture rewards.

Ultimately you don't have to worry too much about the kind of education that draws you in. Education, broadly defined, is one of the best forms of brain food out there. Pursue what you enjoy, and learning can be a lifelong source of interest, personal growth, and fun.

MENTAL REST IS BEST, GET YOUR SLEEP

Now, with all those new things to study all the time, you could go on forever nonstop, right? Wrong! Just as you'd need to take time to recuperate after running a marathon or rest up after a regular day of going to work, shopping, or other tasks, if you don't get enough sleep, your mind will be compromised. Sleep hits the "reset" button in your brain. No matter how energetic you are, sleep is a vital component to your well-being and ability to be effective.

Busy people sometimes say they wish they didn't have to sleep. Some even think sleeping is being lazy or wasting time. We might as well just get used to it—there's no getting around the need for sleep. You might take an energy shot or fill up on coffee on occasion, but you can't pull all-nighters forever.

Here's a thought worth pondering: getting enough sleep is ultimately a time saver rather than a time waster. A well-rested person will get more done—and in much finer fashion—than a sleepy, over-caffeinated person trying to push through.

The next time you berate yourself for wanting to sleep for eight hours, consider your pet cat. Our feline friends sleep twelve hours a day. Don't have a cat? Your dog snoozes ten hours every day. But the sleeping champion is the bat—they customarily nod off for a whopping twenty hours every day!

Perhaps you aspire to be a giraffe and sleep only three or four hours a day.

Those of you who think you're doing nothing while asleep will be interested to know that the body is actually taking care of a lot of business during this most important time. REM sleep—the time associated with dreaming—is the stage most often talked about. However, 75 to 80 percent of sleep is non-REM. During that time breathing decreases, as does the blood pressure, and the heart slows down as well. This non-REM stage is broken down further into four stages—two periods of light sleep and two periods of deep sleep. During these latter two stages of non-REM, growth hormone and the all-important interleukins for building the immune system are released.

REM sleep takes up the other 20 to 25 percent of the sleep cycle. During this time, there is intense mental activity. Breathing, blood pressure, and heart rate all speed up again while the skeletal muscles go into a state of paralysis. When you wake up and remember you'd just been flying or driving a bus through the streets of ancient Rome, or that you had gone to chemistry class and suddenly realized you'd forgotten your pants, you are recalling the dream times that occur during the REM stage.

Together these stages make up one sleep cycle that lasts about ninety minutes. Most adults ideally should get in four to six sleep cycles nightly, or seven to nine hours of sleep. The amount of sleep needed varies somewhat and is determined by each person's genetic makeup, but few people function well on less than six hours.

A high ROI on sleep will give you a focused mind that's able to retain what you learn, a healthy body that is given time to repair itself from daily wear, and energy to pursue your activities with gusto. Your ROI on sleep goes down rapidly when you're not getting enough shut-eye. Without enough sleep, you run the risk of developing fatigue, gaining weight, increasing blood pressure, and increasing blood sugar, and it even raises the risks of heart attack and depression. Other mental changes include short attention span, crankiness, irritability, temperamental attitude, and memory impairment. In addition, becoming drowsy at inappropriate times from lack of sleep can be a major safety risk, especially while driving.

So what is the best way to get your very vital good night's sleep? Try starting with creating the right environment. Maintain your bedroom as a comfortable space. Take the time to pick out just the right mattress and pillows that you can sink into and in which you feel completely at ease. Working, eating, watching TV, or even reading in bed can start to complicate the space. Save those activities for other places in the house. Don't fall asleep outside of the bedroom. If you do, turn in as soon as possible. Your bedroom should be a personal oasis, reserved for sleep and intimate relations.

For four to six hours before bedtime, avoid any type of caffeine. This includes chocolate, coffee, tea, soda, and even some over-the-counter drugs. If you have recurring problems getting to sleep, consider consuming these items only before noon. Some substances that we sometimes think relax us in reality block deep relaxation. Nicotine, for example, is a stimulant that can contribute to sleep difficulties. Alcohol, often thought of as a nightcap, may indeed induce sleep in the beginning but interferes with the deep sleep stages if taken with any regularity within that four- to six-hour timeframe. The late-evening drinking habit can lead to waking in the night more often, and less restful sleep overall.

If you do have trouble falling asleep and think you've eliminated all potential problems, consider what you're eating. A tiny snack before bedtime is fine, but a heavy meal too late at night is often problematic. Heartburn at night does not make for a peaceful sleep time.

Forcing it doesn't quite work, so sleep only when you are drowsy. Try to avoid naps during the day. If you are really exhausted on occasion, limit daytime power naps to one hour. Creating a set bedtime and a set rising time can help the body settle into a regular sleep rhythm.

Avoid strenuous activity within six hours of going to sleep— don't save going to the gym to the last part of the day. Avoid light, loud noise, and extreme temperatures in the bedroom. Sometimes even the use of an alarm clock can have too negative an impact. Consider using a gentle, chiming, Zen alarm clock or something similar, or abandon the wake-up clock ritual altogether if you are able. Remember, your bedroom is your oasis. Give it the right conditions, and as you incorporate more positive, sleep-regulating habits, good rest should follow.

If for whatever reason you can't fall asleep, leave the bedroom and engage in another activity somewhere else. If all the basic methods fail at a significant rate, you may have an underlying medical condition that is preventing good sleep. Between your doctor and any sleep study to which you have access, you may discover you are dealing with obstructive sleep apnea, narcolepsy, restless leg syndrome, disturbed circadian rhythms, or some other obstacle to sleep.

REMEDIES FOR INSOMNIA

Starting at home, there are some things you can do to resolve the problem of insomnia. Do your best to sort out the source of your sleep difficulty, and then follow the advice of a medical professional. Some remedies he or she may prescribe include the use of melatonin or herbals, light therapy, or chronotherapy, and he or she might offer useful tips such as taking a hot bath in the evening.

Melatonin

Our circadian rhythms are the inner time clocks that tell us when it's time to wake and sleep. Jetlag and travel in general, or working the night shift, are among the circumstances that can upset our circadian rhythms.

The hormone melatonin is naturally produced by our bodies. It is secreted in the dark and suppressed in the daylight. When your exposure to light and dark is changed, or you travel across time zones, the system shifts. As a corrective, you may want to take three to five milligrams of melatonin at sunset, several hours before sleep. Depending on where you are, 6:00 p.m. may be good timing.

Chronotherapy

A simple but gradual process, chronotherapy works to change the sleep pattern. Through incremental changes, the sleep and waking times are shifted so the desired pattern is achieved. This method may be used to make a shift over approximately three hours.

Light Therapy

The human body responds to light. Light boxes simulate sunlight and are set to come on at dawn. They can be of great use for awakening those suffering with sleep disturbances and helping to reset the pattern.

The light output is measured as the amount of lux, which is the unit of measurement of the intensity of light falling on a given area. Ten thousand lux is equivalent to natural indirect sunlight. Light boxes can cost anywhere from $300 to $500 each, but if real relief from a persistent sleep disturbance is the result, it is well worth the investment.

Herbs

Valerian is said to be a mild sedative and is used to help induce and improve the quality of sleep. Chamomile, a daisy-like plant whose dried flowers are commonly used as an herbal tea, is good to try in the evening to bring on drowsiness. Passion flower, a perennial climbing vine, is another plant that has been used in teas and various formulas to combat insomnia and anxiety.

Sometimes certain scents can help provide the right environment for sleep. The pleasant aroma of lavender in a diffuser, potpourri, eye pillow, or other imaginative form can be used for this purpose.

Hot Bath

Now here is one that should feel good just about any time. Warm water causes passive body heat and raises the core body temperature. This can help you fall asleep more easily and can allow for more complete periods of the all-important deep sleep. It is always healing to take some time for yourself, draw a bath, and relax. Even if you don't have an immediate problem with sleep, after this indulgence you may be surprised by how much more peaceful your rest time is.

DON'T MESS WITH STRESS

The wonderful thing about the human brain is that we can use it to create just about anything. The terrible thing about the human brain is that we can use it to create just about anything. For all the amazing technological innovations and cultural contributions our minds can think of, we are also quite adept at generating unrealistic expectations, anxieties, and all sorts of pressures that do us no good at all. Stress is a destructive force that lowers the ROI on mental health. Finding strategic ways to get the jump on it will improve your life dramatically.

Stress is a behavioral response—usually a self-initiated reaction to external factors. Its insidious impulse starts in the mind, and then creates a chain reaction of physiological responses including increased heart rate, increased breathing, increased blood sugar, and poor digestion. Unfortunately that's when it's only getting started—how about adding muscle tension, depression, increased risks of heart attack and stroke, premature aging, and decreased cognitive ability?

Fatigue and disturbed sleep patterns are on the list, too, and we've just learned how bad those are for us. The list goes on. Stress contributes to lowered immunity, memory lapses, substance abuse, elevated cholesterol, and trouble in relationships. It actually brings about a condition by which blood is shifted from higher cerebral centers to lower. Essentially, if you are operating in "fight or flight" mode, you wind up in a situation where you can't think straight.

Need I go on? It should be abundantly clear that if you want to maximize your ROI on intellectual and mental health, reducing stress must be a priority.

We rarely think of it this way, but stress also has an aspect that reveals a positive ROI. It acts as a form of protection and a performance booster in crisis situations. So if you need to get away from a dangerous individual or race out of a burning building, a stress response and its subsequent burst of energy can be lifesaving.

The low ROI aspect of stress is by far the more familiar form. The long list of problems associated with stress, like depression, anger, and fear, come from the prolonged variety. In that scenario we usually are experiencing some perception of a long-term lack of control in our lives.

I hope it is encouraging for you to know that we really and truly do have full control over our responses to the stressors in our lives. It is hard to imagine at first, because it feels like so much is thrown our way. Serious changes that trigger stress reactions are bound to happen—you may have a separation or divorce, lose a job, or experience other financial issues, or undergo serious illness or injury. You might get married or retire; and sadly, we all eventually have to deal with the loss of loved ones.

One big step you can take to manage stress is to recognize fully its inevitability. Your mother or your best friend or your kid will do something that upsets you. You'll get frustrated with your boss's attitude. Whatever the incident, something will happen, whether it's a big, life-changing event or a small annoyance, that will make your day feel less than perfect. Finding a way of accepting this reality is wonderfully helpful. When you're not blindsided by stress, you are able to develop tools to help you deal with it.

RELIEVING STRESS

What is the best kind of stress relief for you? You may already know that your favorite sport or getting away to your favorite beach does wonders for you. Maybe a combination of intentional stress-relieving activities does the trick. Consider trying these ideas, alone or in combination, to calm your nerves and get yourself back on track:

- **Meditation**: Find a quiet place, sit still on a cushion or in a chair with your feet flat on the floor, and focus inward on your breath, a mantra, or an affirmation.

- **Mindfulness**: Similar to meditation, it is a state of awareness when one is sharply attuned to the present and thus living in that moment. When you are mindful, you are aware of what is going on in your body, mind, and in the world around you.

- **Deep breathing**: Taking time to sit and breathe deeply for a set period of time or even stopping to take a few deep breaths in the middle of a stressful situation can shift you to a positive, relaxed attitude.

- **Creative arts therapy**: Performing music, drawing, or otherwise making something may help express and/or neutralize feelings of stress.

- **Animal-assisted therapy**: Petting a cat or dog, or even watching fish swim in an aquarium can lower blood pressure and facilitate a sense of calm.

- **Massage**: Muscle tension is a common symptom of stress, and releasing some of that tension helps the body feel better and may begin to melt away negative perceptions in the mind.

- **Aromatherapy**: Pleasant floral, citrus, or other aromas may be used to create a relaxing environment.

- **Light therapy**: Poor sleep patterns, as mentioned earlier, as well as seasonal affective disorder may be corrected with light therapy, thus bringing about a more balanced mental state.

- **Intentions**: By intending or focusing on something, you can set your mind to achieve a goal or dream. An intentional distraction is a way of doing something just to get your mind off it. This seems like old-school advice, but it still has staying power. Try taking a hot bath, going to the park, checking out the bookstore or library, taking a class, joining a club, cooking, hiking, biking, watching a movie, or just stepping out to get some fresh air.

In addition, two important ways to relieve stress are using progressive muscle relaxation and visual imagery. Both methods require you to find a quiet place where you can get out of the way of any immediate stressors. Give yourself some "me" time to try these:

- **Progressive muscle relaxation**: Find a place to sit or lie down comfortably. If you lie down, put a pillow under your head and one beneath you to support your lower back. Close your eyes and breathe deeply. Beginning with the feet and ankles, tense up those muscle groups. Hold the tension for seven to ten seconds, then release, allowing the feet and ankles to go completely limp. Move up the body from there to the calves, thighs, trunk, chest, and arms, all the way to the forehead and scalp. Tense and release each area's muscle groups as you go. Complete the cycle over the course of five to ten minutes, and you should feel a discernible difference in your level of stress.

- **Visual imagery**: This is similar to progressive muscle relaxation. Instead of focusing on muscles, this time focus on a pleasant thought while taking deep, controlled breaths. For those five to ten minutes, notice every sensation related to this pleasant thought. If you imagine yourself on the beach or in a peaceful forest, feel the warmth on your skin, notice what the air smells like, hear the birds nearby, and see the waves or the rustling leaves. Allow yourself to bring every sense into the experience for the best positive effect.

Most people experience times when they feel overwhelmed by stress. At such times, it may help to look toward people who clearly have mastered effective ways to deal with stress. Surgeons and airline pilots must know a thing or two about it—in both professions, panic is not an option.

How do we get to that place? First expect the unexpected. Surgeons know one operation is never exactly the same as another, and neither are everyday life situations. Prepare your mind to deal with many different scenarios, and you will find a way to be comfortable anywhere.

Next, learn to look at your personal stressors as challenges rather than problems. That way you will be energized to make changes that will enhance your mental wellness.

Finally, be willing to learn from your mistakes. A pilot undergoes many hours of training and getting things wrong so that eventually a sense of confidence and a cool hand will prevail. Do the same with your life. A sure way to anxiety is to continue heading down the roads that led you there in the first place. Make changes, use the relaxation tools that work for you, and you will feel more stress-free and happy.

SELF-ESTEEM: WHO DO YOU SEE IN THE MIRROR?

What is self-esteem? Simply put, it is how you perceive yourself when you look in the mirror. Do you feel good about the person you see there? Do you feel angry or ashamed? How you feel about yourself directly or indirectly affects your mood, attitudes, thoughts, decision making, and relationships, and your overall ROI on intellectual and mental health.

Good self-esteem doesn't mean having a big ego. In reality it is quite the opposite. People with healthy self-esteem have an innate sense of security, which actually allows them to see and accept their own imperfections. However, people with low self-esteem tend to have distorted views of themselves. Whether someone comes off as an overstuffed peacock or a shrinking violet, a distorted self-perception because of low self-esteem usually has little to do with what others actually think of that person. Whether positive or negative, the attitudes associated with self-esteem usually are the products of a lifetime, and they imprint on the fabric of the mind. Since these attitudes can be either strongly fulfilling or counterproductive, it is useful to learn how to maximize the positive. To get there let's look a little more closely at what is *not* representative of good self-esteem.

You may have a negative ROI on self-esteem if self-confidence becomes overconfidence and boils over into arrogance. You may exhibit an unhealthy self-centered attitude, or in extreme cases, outright narcissism. With an inflated sense of self, it is difficult for people like this to accept constructive criticism. This creates poor relationships all around.

A hallmark of low self-esteem is blaming external factors and other people for your problems. Continuing to feel negatively about your situation and others in the environment can both originate from and/or begin to generate the most self-defeating thoughts.

Fear is another big factor. Fear of rejection and fear of loneliness can drive your mind into dark places and lead you to poor decision making. Anxiety, depression, and anger can set in, and in the extreme these have the power to destroy not only your mental health but all your other Core Assets as well.

Some attitudes, when expressed outwardly, may indicate that you are operating out of low self-esteem. When you blame others directly for your problems, it is a clear sign of low self-esteem. You don't have to look at yourself so closely when you externalize issues in this way. Blowing potentially negative situations out of proportion is another common mechanism. If you make a proverbial mountain out of a molehill, the focus on you and your attitudes is deflected. Focusing on the negative in general is a typical feature of this type of thinking.

Other expressions of self-esteem issues can come out in slightly different manifestations, including thinking in extremes. Black-and-white thinking creates beliefs that say, "It's either one thing or the other" and "It's all or nothing." This doesn't leave space in the psyche for the subtlety required to look for helpful changes or creative solutions. Neither does jumping to conclusions, feelings of intense jealously, an undue sense of entitlement, or the rigid insistence on exactitude brought on by perfectionism. Sometimes an overblown ego gives way to the opposite situation, in which people are sure that much of what they have done is wrong. If you are experiencing the "shoulda coulda woulda" syndrome, it may lead you to dwell sadly or angrily on what you think you ought to have done.

Most healthy minds are capable of entering one or more of these realms from time to time. However, when these thought or behavior patterns become reflexive and continual, it becomes problematic. When you develop good habits of self-reflection, you can help soften the effects of a tendency toward acting out from a place of low self-esteem.

With the mind's ability to weave such unpleasant webs, how does anyone begin to get over the distorted realities generated by low self-esteem? If you have been suffering in any of these ways, the first thing to do is recognize the problem. It may be easier said than done; that is true of many things in life. But starting somewhere is the key. You have the ability to shift your perceptions. Don't avoid it—own up to it and get to work.

It could take some time, especially if the blame game has been at work. But eventually you may be able to begin asking, "Why do I *really* feel this way?" Unraveling the sources of insecurity through self-examination is a move in the direction of healing. Employing one or more of the techniques for stress relief may be helpful. Your chance for insight may emerge when you slow down the spinning wheels in your mind.

Once you begin to ask questions, you can move to the next phase: getting to know yourself. Explore who you are inside—your likes, your dislikes, and the values that drive your actions in the world. Most of all, get to know your foibles and even what you may see as your shortcomings. Get comfortable in your own skin. You don't have to be the person you think your mother wanted you to be or the person you want the public to believe you are. Recognize your own uniqueness, and you will discover unlimited potential.

Learn to understand the phrase "it is what it is." In many ways this simple idea is very true. We all have our characteristics and so does every other person and every situation in the world. There are so many factors over which we have no control, and it can be a challenge to differentiate what you can change from what you can't. The best policy is to take stock of who you are and what you are contributing to the world, change what you can for the better, and accept the rest.

As you wind your way through greater self-awareness, you will get to the place of realizing that no one is perfect. The perfectionist is the only one in need of constant approval. The ways in which you diverge from the norm in some way are the very traits people tend to appreciate and admire in others. If you deal with your perceived imperfections in a healthy way, that experience builds character and makes you stronger mentally.

When low self-esteem has you trying to hide your imperfections and shortcomings, life becomes stressful. The energy expended to keep secrets and hold back thoughts and feelings makes daily living exhausting. It is no wonder that when people share their imperfections, they feel like a big weight has been lifted from their shoulders.

Ultimately only you can help yourself reap the highest possible ROI on self-esteem. Many methods are out there to transition negative feelings to positive ones. Here is one I recommend: Take a leap of faith and share an honest moment with someone. Try telling someone about a trait of yours that you think is an imperfection. Sharing is a sign of strength, not weakness. It shows humbleness, earns respect, and makes friends. It is an act of high self-esteem and self-confidence. This simple moment of humility will help you get stronger in the all-important ability to respect and love yourself no matter the circumstance.

A WORD ABOUT INTUITION

There are a host of other authors out there who can tell you a great deal about how to develop intuition. I will leave most of the details to them, but I do want to mention that intuitive thinking is very much a part of strong and healthy intellectual development. Learning to use intuition gives you a way of tapping into the subconscious mind. It is learning how to move in the world with a kind of built-in gut feeling. Your intuition can give you an edge when you learn to heed its subtle messages.

In our usual daily lives, we gather information about the world around us through all our senses. Becoming more intuitive seems to have something to do with keeping your mind especially open to all that external stimuli that comes your way. That information usually sits idly in our subconscious minds and is processed while we pay attention to other things.

Sometimes, when we need a little extra push of awareness or a better way of understanding a situation, we can tap into that idle information. Our subconscious reservoir manifests itself more consciously. It becomes an "aha" moment or a hunch.

Keep an open mind about intuition. Diversify the input your brain receives through having varied experiences. I don't mean spend more time in information overload on the Internet, but have an extra moment to take in the sights, sounds, and smells wherever you go. Be vigilant and observant. Get out of the house and take in the conversations you hear in your travels.

The best time to absorb external stimuli is when the mind is in a state of relaxation and calm. After a while you may find yourself just knowing when you ought to bring extra business cards to a party or which job offer to take. You may sense that vacationing on Martha's Vineyard may be somehow better for you next summer than heading to the Outer Banks. You might follow your sudden impulse to talk to the girl in the teal hat after class. You never know what will happen when you really pay attention—one or more of those instances may lead you to exactly where you need to be.

CAPS FOR ROI ON INTELLECTUAL, EMOTIONAL, AND MENTAL HEALTH

The equally wonderful and challenging thing about learning and mental health is that you can always seek to know more and to be even clearer, more focused, and more aware. The following **C**ORE **A**SSET **P**ROTECTION **S**TRATEGIES offer a few more tips to help you along.

1. **Simplify.** Declutter your office. Finally get rid of the clothes you've been meaning to give away. Implement the best system that gets the dishes done and keeps the laundry pile at bay. Cleanliness and good organization skills will help you feel focused and in a good mental state. And as it is on the outside, let it be on the inside as well.

   Declutter your brain. Think of it like clearing your mental cache just like a computer cache. When you're through organizing your house, take a day off to give your mind a rest. Do something simple and enjoyable. Releasing old energies and information will lead to the brain's running more smoothly and efficiently.

2. **Avoid information overload.** Here is where you can take simplifying to a new level. You will not have to spend so much time decluttering your surroundings and your brain if you set clear boundaries around what information you will take in and when. Maybe you will choose not to turn on the computer at all on Saturday or Sunday. You may decide that the news channel reporting on fires, murders, and scandals is not what you need to watch. The time you spend in one day telling companies to stop sending junk mail will save you countless hours of feeling obligated to go through it all. Just because most people around you respond to text messages during dinner or in the middle of a heartfelt conversation

doesn't mean you have to join the club. Let the Information Age work for you rather than allowing it to control your time and energy.

3. **Unleash your creative thinking.** We all have some degree of it. Why not tap into that inner creativity? Getting there means turning away from the well-worn paths and letting go of any fear you may have to explore opportunities and take chances. Some educators and institutions keep attempting to keep us reined in, and this teaches many of us simply to tow the line. Real intellectual and creative discovery comes from breaking away from that pattern.

   So go ahead—get out of your comfort zone. If you have an idea that's different, have fun with it. Let it come naturally. Take time away from it when you need to, and come back when it calls. You just may be on to something.

4. **Keep visualizing your goals.** Visualizing yourself meeting your positive goals truly can help you realize success. Do this frequently. At least once a day, conjure the imagery in your mind that gives you the feeling you've reached the pinnacle. By keeping your goals in the forefront of your brain and giving them distinct pictures, you will stay committed to your aspirations and dreams. Visualization improves your chances if you use it to focus yourself on success.

5. **Use affirmations.** You may feel silly at first, but give it a chance. Taking the time to do visualizations might be hard enough for some people, but taking this extra step might really nail it for you. Learn to use repeated statements of positive reinforcement to support your goals. Keep them short, sweet, and to the point:

"I am at peace."

"My mind is calm and relaxed."

"I will win."

Even if you're not sure whether these statements are true, keep at it, and they will do their work.

6. **It's okay to fail.** Of course you want to get it right the first time, but that's not always the way it goes. The fear of failure is a primary reason people don't try things in the first place.

   Letting go of that fear or allowing yourself to continue on in the face of fear are great boons for mental health. It feels good to move on to the realization of ideas. The brain gets exercise solving the new puzzles you're willing to put before it. And yes, you will sometimes learn from your mistakes.

   Understand that life and pet projects will always have setbacks and disappointments. Regroup and come back fighting on another day. Persist, don't desist.

7. **Have forgiveness.** Holding on to negative emotions does no one any good. Denying these feelings is not healthy, either. The balanced response is to feel your feelings and then find the ability to let them go.

   Dealing with other human beings is often a messy business, and feelings will get hurt. If you think someone has done you wrong, it is perfectly normal to feel anger, sadness, and indignation. In time, allow yourself to move on. Your own mental health will thank you for leaving the negativity behind.

8. **Don't underestimate yourself.** Many of us have been taught to keep quiet or not to believe in ourselves. Try your best to forget those misguided lessons. People learn by speaking

up and asking questions. You won't know about your talents and intellectual capacities without trying, so go for it! Then be proud of your strengths. Maximize and appreciate them while you work on your weaknesses. Keep your mind moving, and your best will get even better.

9. **Laugh!** Don't ever let anyone tell you that laughter, humor, and light-heartedness are frivolous and unnecessary. On the contrary, laughter has an amazing ability to improve overall wellness. The professor who adds a joke here and there to his lectures is the one whose students recall years after they've left his classes. Humor creates good moods, and good moods keep people in healthy states of mind.

There are so many reasons a pleasant attitude is good for you, but sometimes you don't even need to review the many psychological and even physical benefits. Laughter feels good. Enjoy it and you will enjoy life.

6

Love and Happiness:
Your ROI on Relationships

LIFE SHARED IS A LIFE FULFILLED

Humans are social beings by nature. Forming good relationships is among the most difficult and most rewarding things you can do. Love, affection, companionship, friendship, and other variations on closeness are necessary for our well-being and touch us to our deepest core. Poets and scientists alike continue to search for the perfect way to describe or evoke the experience of love and connection. The jury may always be out on singular definitions, but one thing is sure: we need each other.

Usually, when relationships come to mind, people immediately think of the romantic sort. There is the puppy love in elementary school and the major crushes that carry us into high school. Once we start dating, most of us get a full range of experiences from good to bad to ugly. I definitely had my share of disaster dates along with the fun and memorable ones.

While dating and romantic love are certainly important to the majority of us, the many ways of interacting with others are also important. The closest of those relationships are vital to life. Other, more extended relationships are still essential and serve to hold together the fabric of our societies.

I have learned a lot about life through trial, error, and observation, and relationships have certainly been a part of that. I used to get easily flustered in social situations. For me, learning the ropes of networking in the business world hasn't always been the simplest task. I've gotten stuck in embarrassing situations, such as forgetting names and faces, neglecting to follow up after important conversations, and other blunders. I've seen the dark side of relationships, such as when a devastating divorce leaves a family in ruins, and friends are forced to choose sides. I have experienced loneliness enough to realize the true value of companionship. In those times I began to understand the concept of solitary confinement. How terrible a punishment it must be to lose not only your freedom but also the social contact so inherent to the human experience.

Despite the ups and downs, I have come to lead a life rich with friends and family. My work relationships have grown solid, and I live in a neighborhood with people I trust. Since I have lived in several different cities, I've made friendships across the country that I expect to stand the test of time. All in all, when it comes to relationships, I consider myself truly blessed.

A very useful way to look at the structure of relationships in our lives is to think of an onion. It has many layers, just like the circles in which we associate. The inner core of our connections is comprised of our best friends, lovers, and immediate family. Most likely this is a haven for only five to ten people in your life. In this inner core you encounter your most significant emotional experiences.

Once you move out from the core, the middle layers of your onion represent a large percentage of the people you know. These aren't your most important confidantes, but these are friends with whom you seek to spend a regular amount of quality time. Aunts, uncles, cousins, and other extended family members usually have middle-layer places in our lives.

You might envision the next outer layer as being made up of current and former colleagues. These are the people you work with or, if you are a student or teacher, the ones who share your academic environment.

Neighbors are another layer. You live nearby, and thus feel a common bond. You may help rake their yard on occasion, and they may share a meal from time to time.

After that come the communities through which you travel. These may include religious organizations, ethnic affinities, and special interest groups like a writers' group or an investment club.

The outermost layer represents your acquaintances. It is tempting to believe that someone you see at the coffee shop once in a while is inconsequential, but even these simple, more distant relationships play roles in how you construct your sense of belonging. After all, an onion with only a core would be missing many of its subtle flavors. An onion with only an outer layer would be hollow. Sometimes the wise words of your best friend may feel like the only thing that matters. On another day a smile from the guy who is always working behind the counter at the hardware store might make all the difference.

The nature of relationship dynamics does a very good job of giving credence to the saying "the only thing constant is change." No matter how much you may want some of them to stay exactly the same, your relationships are never static. Are all the relationships you had ten years ago exactly the same today? The chances of that being the case are rather low. By the same token, ten years from now you can expect friends and acquaintances to have again shifted significantly. You will lose touch with some people while others will move closer to becoming core connections.

Working through all layers of the onion today is the web of social networking. No discussion on contemporary relationships would be complete without it. The impact of Facebook, Twitter, and myriad other Internet and social media sites is nothing short of revolutionary. Texting also contributes to the prevalence of instantaneous communication at any time of day or night. The high ROI of being plugged in 24/7, which includes making and rediscovering friends, the exploration of ideas, and business networking, can be counteracted by problems like time consumption, privacy concerns, and ironically, decreased communication skills. Do we want to continue on a path that reduces the art of the love note to this?

OMG, gr8 2 c u last wk! I rly like u. C u agn irl?
Idk, mayb 2mrrow?

I am not suggesting we turn back the clock on social networking, even if that were possible. You may land your next job or meet your next great love online. I do want to stress that no online chat or text speak can take the place of face-to-face interaction and nuanced conversation. I focus on real-life relationship building in this chapter.

WHY MAKE THE REAL RELATIONSHIP EFFORT?

We all know people who seem more interested in distancing them-selves from others rather than in forming relationships. You may have seen this in a loner kid who never wanted to sit with anyone in the cafeteria at school. Maybe you had a boss who preferred to rule with fear rather than friendliness. And what about that friend who finds a reason to break off each new romance three weeks into it for no apparent reason?

Psychology is complex, and there is no telling why some of those patterns arise. It would be unfair to say such tendencies are always bad. However, it is true that people have an inherent need to be loved and ultimately want to seek relationships with others.

The ROI on relationships is virtually unlimited. Life is a whole lot easier when there are supportive people there to listen when times are difficult, to push you gently toward achieving your goals, to share celebrations, and to care enough to cocreate a safe and lov-ing home. Stress is often markedly reduced for people who main-tain strong connections. Communicating with others when there are likely to be few clashes and misunderstandings leads to a greater chance of overall wellness. Studies have even shown that babies who aren't held and cuddled have higher rates of abnormal development and illness. It is clear that even from birth, good times spent with others help us grow in every way.

As children we begin to consciously desire good relationships if only, at first, to get Mom to think well enough of us to give us an extra dessert or treat. Relationships help you get what you want. As your ties grow beyond immediate family, the depth and com-plexity of your relationships do too. Even though they can begin, evolve, and change all by themselves, good relationships do take work. Strong, healthy bonds with others require risk taking, courage, energy, sincerity, honesty, and appreciation. It takes time and effort to learn how to strengthen ties with others to achieve the best outcome for all. Ultimately, what you put into forming and maintaining relationships is what you'll get out of them.

FIRST STEPS TO GOOD COMMUNICATION

It all begins with you. Your self-esteem has a direct effect on the success of a relationship. And while your self-esteem is the product of many forces—some of which are beyond your control, such as how your parents treated you—it is a personal quality that you have the power to shape.

Don't dwell on your past failures; if you're thinking about your history of breakups, your divorce from your first spouse, or any other upsetting circumstance, you will probably project little confidence when meeting new people. Past negatives shouldn't be allowed to get in the way of new opportunities. If you find you need to address any fears, anger, or depression, give yourself the gift of personal growth work that you need. Start out seeking new connections while feeling good about yourself, and stay present in the moment.

Remember that the person you are meeting, whether in a social or business context, may very well be just as nervous as you are. They may be wondering what to say, or are afraid they have forgotten your name, or are concerned that they won't make a good impression. You have the opportunity to put them at ease. You can be the one who takes the lead and helps make your new acquaintance feel comfortable.

Timing is everything. When you are about to approach someone for the first time, have you taken a moment to notice his or her mood? Emotions are so complex that it is virtually impossible to know exactly how another person feels, especially on short order. Nevertheless, by becoming aware of common cues, you can learn quite a bit. When you initiate contact, do you receive a half smile or a face turned away in disinterest? If so, it may be prudent to wait until another time to engage in conversation. Do you get positive feedback, like smiling and eye contact? In that case it might just be the time to strike up a beautiful friendship.

They say overexposure is a bad thing, but I believe *under*exposure is the bigger problem when it comes to making a connection. If, for example, you've developed a bit of a crush on someone, what better way to create an opportunity for a positive response than by letting that person in on the secret? By spending time around the person and respectfully expressing your interest, you are more likely to receive a positive response than you would if you disappear into the wall whenever the person walks into the room. When people know that you like them, their subconscious mind gives them a boost toward liking you back.

Talk less, listen more. Be confident, not cocky. Have a sense of humor. So much of this advice might be summed up with clever slogans, but there is a lot of truth to the old sayings. Let's get beyond these basics, though, for a look at some of the major skills needed for relationship building. Both verbal and nonverbal communication is happening all the time. Familiarize yourself with how to navigate the cues we give one another, and chances are you'll be on your way to something good.

VERBAL COMMUNICATION

Verbal communication is at its best when there is an easygoing sense of openness, honesty, and respect. A common tendency when meeting someone new is to be on your toes, saying whatever it takes to make a good first impression. It may not be easy, but try to relax a little. Typical first date conversations are often rife with equivocation and clever quips that sound like they might have been over-rehearsed. If you keep only one guideline in mind about high-ROI verbal communication, remember to keep it real.

In our context this doesn't mean posing as whatever current pop culture says is hip. It means being you. A good way to start is to allow yourself to be assertive. At first this may sound unattractive, but assertiveness shows confidence. Being able to show up with a sense of self-assurance is a very healthy quality to have, whether it's applied to meeting someone for the first time or woven into the fabric of a lifelong love. It helps you to say "yes" or "no" with clarity, so expressing your thoughts and intentions becomes easier. Assertive people can discuss issues and find they disagree without feeling threatened or descending into personal attacks. Unlike aggressiveness, which is characterized by a mean-spirited intent to dominate or force your will on someone else, assertiveness is speaking from your own power and choice.

Especially when you're feeling the dreamy spark of new romance, compliments seem to flow forth effortlessly. It is good news, then, that giving compliments actually is an effective form of communication in nearly any friendly situation. We may not generally admit it, but most of us revel in being paid a compliment. A sincere compliment serves to empower someone else through words of appreciation, encouragement, and support.

The best compliments are those that are specific and straight from the heart. By letting someone know specifically what you like about them, you will avoid sounding like you are using cookie-cutter phrases that have been uttered thousands of times or engaging in empty flattery. Speak about an aspect of the person that you truly admire. Smile and use the person's name.

The business of giving compliments can be a little tricky. Not enough and you may find you are holding back a good portion of your feelings when you like someone. Too many, especially in the very beginning, and the object of your appreciation will feel bombarded. You don't have to give a flowery description of how you love someone's hair, eyes, laugh, political views, and math skills all in the same five-minute conversation. Let it flow and realize the need for positive feedback will grow as a relationship grows. Allow yourself to compliment your friend more frequently as you spend more time together.

Compliments work both ways. When you receive one, it's best simply to accept it with grace. If you send it right back—by saying, "Oh, I like your outfit, too," for example—it sounds disingenuous. Not accepting a compliment at all is a sign of poor self-esteem. Keep it all on a positive note and just say, "Thank you."

Despite all our defenses, people really do want to open up. What could be more attractive than a friendly, open person? Tell your new friend some things about yourself, your family, your interests, or your community. There's no need for heavy-hitting topics right off the bat. Topics that are reasonably engaging and based on your real interests are ideal. Talking with a person who is not afraid to let his or her guard down invites the same openness in others.

To enhance this experience, consider using open-ended questions. I don't mean overly general queries like "How's life?" or "What's up?" More specific conversation points allow the other person to know you are interested. "How do you plan to develop the new business idea you mentioned?" or "What are some of the things you enjoyed about the theater?" invite thoughtful responses, show you're interested, and keep the conversation going.

Getting to know someone new can be scary. None of us has 100 percent confidence all the time. One of the mechanisms we sometimes use to guard ourselves is to be less than forthcoming. We think, "If I don't talk about that less-than-perfect issue, he or she will like me just fine." Once again, hiding doesn't work. Be open, and your connections will be more genuine.

As you practice the art of conversation, you will discover patterns that lead to positive results. Adjusting your vocabulary to be more similar to the vocabulary of the person you're speaking with can make for a comfortable, productive discussion. Being concise and efficient with your words is also helpful. And for Pete's sake, think before you talk. Blurting something out before your brain has fully engaged might spell trouble.

High-ROI verbal communication projects assertiveness and openness and conveys compliments with sincerity. Becoming a sensitive conversationalist also means paying attention to the feedback from the other person. Is she asking you to rephrase your question? Did his answer make a good point to keep the conversation lively? Feedback may come in words, but it also may show up in another way we communicate—in the form of nonverbal cues.

NONVERBAL COMMUNICATION

Nonverbal communication is every bit as important as refining your gift of gab. Believe it or not, more than 90 percent of our communication is nonverbal, so understanding what your body language is saying about you can help you make that all-important first impression. Important physical cues include eye contact, positive nodding, smiling, appropriate touching, gesturing and positioning, and use of personal space and distance.

The most critical nonverbal cue is smiling. A broad, natural smile will win people over and put them at ease. It is most well received when you are completely at ease. Most people also have a more guarded social smile that is most well received when it comes on slowly and appears genuine and trustworthy. A big grin will often seem forced or obligatory.

Another kind of smile is the smirk, which shows up when you are skeptical. Then there is the opposite of smiling—the scowl or frown. Unhappiness, disapproval, and doubt are human emotions as well, so there is nothing wrong with these looks as long as you are aware of them and are confident about what you wish to convey. Keep in mind that happiness and enthusiasm will appeal to more people, and putting a smile on your face will help keep your spirits uplifted through life's tribulations.

It may sound a bit odd, but there's nothing wrong with a little rehearsal. Look in a mirror occasionally and practice your smiles, facial relaxation, and other expressions. Analyze some photos to examine your smile. You will be surprised by what you learn, and you may be inspired to try a new look. Find a smile that matches your inner joy, and new friends just might beat a path to your door.

Eye contact is also a very important mechanism. Making clear eye contact in conversation denotes interest in what the other person is saying. A subtle shift in pupil dilation is telling as well. The more dilated, the more your eyes are saying they like what they see. Dilation sends the subconscious message that something is pleasing and we are feeling an attraction. It is no wonder then that we dim the lights, making the eyes dilate naturally, to set a romantic mood. In an everyday situation, remember to make eye contact for the best overall communication.

Nodding shows agreement. It lets the other party know you understand and approve. Nodding, like eye contact, is also a sign that you are listening intently. If you find you are not nodding at typically appropriate times during a conversation, you are probably conveying confusion, disapproval, or ignorance of the topic at hand.

The importance of the handshake in Western culture is an indication of the power of touch in building relationships. A firm handshake projects confidence and inner strength—two traits that raise your likeability factor. A limp handshake shows weakness and disinterest, while a bone-crushing handshake can be a bit overbearing; neither is likely to help you win friends or nail down a deal.

Other kinds of connection-building touches include a hand on the shoulder or a hug in the proper context. A creepy, uninvited touch will send your ROI through the floorboards, so keep it on the up-and-up for positive responses.

Your overall body position says a great deal about how you're feeling in the given moment. You will project more interest and engagement by sitting up straight than by slouching. If you hold your posture in a closed position, with legs crossed and arms leaning away from the person you're talking with, it reveals disinterest or a lack of approval. An open posture that includes facing the person conveys that you care about what is being said and are respectful of the person saying it.

Try to be mindful of other people's need for space around them. Everyone values his or her own personal space. Though it varies across genders, cultures, and moods, the average space between people is two feet. Among good friends that space can collapse to only one foot. Moving closer still usually conveys intimacy, except when the intent is hostile. Lack of awareness might lead you to move in too close for another person's comfort.

If you are a world traveler or encounter people from many different places, you will discover differences in personal space. Most people from Europe and Latin America have relatively small personal spaces. Middle Easterners are comfortable in even closer spaces. Americans, by contrast, have larger personal spaces, while those from England keep even more distance. These are only a few vague guidelines, so paying attention to body language in regard to personal space is important. If you are talking with someone and you notice them backing away, you may have just crossed the invisible line. Take a small step back to put the person at ease.

WHEN THE GOING GETS TOUGH

With all the things to think about when you want to make a good impression, it might feel like a small miracle when a relationship manages to grow beyond its humble beginnings. Fortunately, with trial, error, and practice, you can learn the arts of conversation and body language that help lead you into relationships. Unfortunately, relationships aren't going to be rosy all of the time.

What do you do when the inevitable conflicts and disagreements arise? Stay calm. Keeping your composure and applying conflict management techniques can save the day. If you allow your personal anxiety to take over, the results may not be what you want.

There are high-ROI and low-ROI responses. First let's look at a few low-ROI responses to conflict. We all have our moments, but if you can manage it, here's what *not* to do:

- **Avoidance**: If you just walk away from a heated situation, it doesn't leave any opportunity for resolution.

- **Shutting down criticism**: If someone has a beef with you, responding with an immediate excuse tells that person you haven't heard the complaint.

- **Firing back**: Meeting anger with anger without listening will only escalate an argument.

- **Denial**: You may be tempted to not even acknowledge a problem or disagreement at all.

High-ROI conflict management takes a calmer disposition. If you need a moment to take a deep breath before trying to resolve an issue, do so. That little pause can really make meaningful interaction possible. Coming to a common understanding with your partner or friend about methods of constructive resolution while all is calm can be a great, proactive way to go. Here are a few examples of effective steps for working through those times when blood pressures are rising:

- **Be specific**. Yelling, "You always do this!" or "You never do that!" is counterproductive. If something has just upset you, try talking about the matter at hand rather than bringing up twenty things from the past. Delving into generalities only muddies the water and invites an attack on things *you* may have done.

- **Analyze the issue**. Once you've determined a single issue, it is much easier to talk it out. Is it a new issue? Is it old? Is it substantiated? The more you share information collaboratively, the better the result. Finding out more about what is bothering you or the other person creates opportunities for changes or improvements if needed.

- **Give response time**. When you give criticism, be silent afterward, no matter how much you may want to launch into "and another thing . . ." Allow the person time to receive, reflect, and respond. Agree that he or she will give you the same courtesy when the direction of the conversation reverses.

- **Admit wrongdoing**. None of us is perfect. Realize that having a disagreement isn't about winning or losing, but growing within a relationship. If someone calls you out on a problem, be prepared to admit to it.

- **Agree to disagree**. Sometimes you'll need to stick to your guns. Realize everyone is entitled to an opinion, and feelings are always valid.

Ultimately, the answer is finding the pathway to forgiveness. It can be difficult, but without it, internal desires for revenge or punishment may be released that, when left unaddressed, can sabotage any relationship beyond repair.

Before you can forgive others, though, you have to learn to forgive yourself. Guilt is a heavy burden to carry around. Acknowledge your pain, and know that the other party has personal demons, too. Make the commitment to do what it takes to release guilt, anger, resentment, and bitterness. Be kind to yourself and those you love, even when you may feel disappointed. Remember it is okay to be human. Push through the pain and find your way back to happiness.

LEARNING TO LISTEN

Absolutely one of the most important skills for good communication is to be a good listener. Some attitudes get in the way of listening, like making rash assumptions; biases based on a person's age, ethnicity, religion, or actions; a lack of focus; or just being too busy talking about yourself. Sometimes people shut down when they are afraid of what they may hear. Sometimes they have selective hearing and listen only to what they want to hear.

If you've grown accustomed to any of these pitfalls, it may take some work to become a listener. You may think you weren't even born with the patience to truly listen. In fact, most of us do have very low retention rates; we recall only about 25 percent of what we hear. No wonder we run into misunderstandings. You are not alone if this skill so far has evaded you. Luckily, active listening is a skill that can be learned.

Here's where those verbal and nonverbal cues come in. If you remember to keep eye contact, hold your body still, and focus on the friend who is speaking, those postures will help that friend know you are listening. At the same time, adopting those outward signs will in turn help you take notice of what your friend is saying. You'll be paying attention. That is what it takes to hear a message with clarity.

Good listening allows time for the other person to speak. Try not to interrupt or fidget in a way that indicates boredom or frustration. If someone is taking the time to give you a message, it must be important to that person. Give your full attention so your friend will feel he or she has expressed the idea fully. Show respect and empathy for his or her feelings.

When you are fully engaged in listening, you are not approaching it from a place of judgment. There is no room for putdowns or ridicule. Hold off on giving advice unless it is requested. Once the other person feels he or she has been heard in an open, nonjudgmental way, he or she will be more interested in you and what you have to say.

All this listening really helps keep conversations going. By being quiet you will be more likely to come back with just the right follow-up question or conversation piece. The back and forth will grow naturally, and you will in turn discover how good it feels to be heard. Give and you shall receive. The better a listener you become, the better your relationships will be.

GETTING INTIMATE

Now we get to those most intimate of relationships. Sex is one of the most compelling human experiences. Through lovemaking, partners discover new levels of closeness and connection. Sorry to disappoint, but this is not going to be about the Kama Sutra or tantra. Having sex is a passionate give and take, a sharing of oneself that is unequalled. Isn't it a great bonus that it also gives us a high ROI on physical benefits?

In case you haven't noticed, sex is a great stress reliever. You may also have noticed that sex can be good exercise: every half hour of doing the wild thing can burn 150 calories. It makes sense then that it also improves cardiovascular health.

Sex boosts our feel-good hormones, endorphins, as well as oxytocin, the body's natural pain reliever, making the activity quite a good antidepressant. Sex can help you feel younger and healthier because it boosts the DHEA levels that keep tissue healing and the immune system in good form.

A poor sexual relationship can cause relationship problems beyond physical frustration. Continued sexual disconnect or the absence of intimacy altogether can lead to emotional pain that starts to magnify other inadequacies in the relationship. Let there be no shame. All aspects of your closest relationships need tending to, so don't take sex for granted. Communicate about your love and your desires. Talk about it, find your groove, keep it spicy, and allow that most wonderful closeness to work its healthy relationship magic.

CAPS FOR ROI ON RELATIONSHIP HEALTH

Keep these **C**ORE **A**SSET **P**ROTECTION **S**TRATEGIES in mind when you are building a new relationship or focusing on keeping a longtime connection alive and well.

1. **Check your baggage.** In order to have healthy relationships, you first have to strive for a healthier you. Bringing your baggage into relationships generates opportunities for conflict, so do your emotional homework. It may help to review the previous chapter as you take steps to strengthen your self-esteem. Your personal growth means happier times with others.

2. **Consider your social wealth.** Just as this whole book looks at the major aspects of life in terms of return on investment, it may be particularly helpful to look at your relationships through this lens. The quality and depth of your relationships are part of your wealth. What is the state of your social wealth? Have you invested enough in your friendships? Your family? Have you concentrated too much on your guys'-night-out crowd and not enough on your office colleagues? Take some time to look at the big picture, and then reallocate your time and energy as needed.

3. **There is such a thing as TMI.** Honesty, at the beginning of any relationship, is a good thing. However, too much information (TMI) is not always the best idea. You don't need to talk about past failed relationships, your hemorrhoids, or the details of your bathroom habits on a first date. Use discretion and common sense. Be open, but you don't have to spill your guts.

4. **Don't be a faker.** Don't pretend to be someone you're not. People aren't that stupid. No one wants to hear you brag about your money, your cars, or your rock-star mansion. And by all means, don't start off a relationship with lies. The longer a lie stays in action, the more it will hurt everyone involved when the truth comes out. If you acknowledge your reality by including your faults rather than hiding them, people will come to appreciate, respect, and accept you even more.

5. **Listen to yourself.** What you say is important, but so is how it sounds. Be aware of your vocal tones. Higher-pitched sounds give off a feeling of anxiousness, while if you use lower tones you'll sound less stressed. Make some recordings at home to practice and analyze what you hear. If the tone of your sentences goes up at the end, you will sound unsure, as if you are asking a question. End your statements with a period to sound more confident.

6. **Learn the art of allowing.** Sometimes relationships need to follow their own timelines. There is no need to start early conversations with super-intense questions. Keep it light at first; use open-ended questions, and allow the conversations to grow on their own into greater complexity. After you speak, leave space to receive a well-considered answer. Stay positive, stay in touch, and if deeper sharing is to happen, it will blossom when the time is right.

7

What Money Can Buy:
Your ROI on Economic Health

THE MANY FACES OF MONEY

What is money? For some people it conjures up negative images of crass greed. For others, chasing the almighty dollar might look like life's most important pursuit. It may be perceived as a source of power, prestige, control, security—a measure of success and achievement, self-worth, ego, or entertainment. Still others may see money as only a simple vehicle to meet their daily needs.

Somewhere within this broad spectrum lies the truth: money is a tool used to achieve a degree of satisfaction, comfort, and fulfillment.

Most people will be able to see fairly easily how money intersects with the majority of the other Core Assets. It can play a key role in achieving physical health, pursuing a good education, maintaining relationships, and ensuring safety. How you perceive and handle it will most likely affect your other Core Assets. If you have a balanced relationship with money, it can more easily enhance the other important aspects of your life. If you are plagued with worries about money, Core Assets including your relationships, mental and physical health, work performance, and personal safety may all suffer.

But we haven't discussed one important Core Asset in relation to money: what about its place in spirituality? There is some debate about this, and many of the great religions and philosophers have shown a wide range of perspectives. St. Paul, for instance, emphatically stated, "The love of money is the root of all evil." Many Buddhist monks were, and still are, forbidden from even touching it. In Islam, Sharia Law prohibits the collection of interest on loans. Orthodox Jews aren't allowed to spend money on the Sabbath. In Hinduism, however, the Goddess Lakshmi is worshipped for her blessings of wealth and prosperity.

Times have changed dramatically. We now live in an Information Age where we are globally connected. The necessities of times past are no longer closely aligned with the necessities of today. I've wondered if Jesus lived in contemporary times, would he need a well-funded retirement plan? Perhaps not, since he would probably have an incredible amount of willing donors to support him. It's hard to imagine him podcasting his message on the Internet, let alone growing up as a youth inundated by video games.

That's how much times have changed. The point is, just because money may have been perceived one way during a previous time, it doesn't mean it's necessarily a bad thing today.

The universal message from the great religions and many philosophers alike is to not let yourself become consumed by money and the pursuit of wealth. They should never be allowed to control your life. Ultimately, money is only a man-made metric that places arbitrary values on both tangible items, like man-made or natural goods, and intangible things like time and labor. Money today has a mostly virtual existence. It only truly exists when you have a few bills and some change in your pocket—that is, when you actually carry it. Everything else simply exists on paper or in computer kilobytes, whether it's a bank statement, a deed, or perhaps stocks and options. Many of the ultrarich rarely even see more than a fraction of their wealth because most of it exists on paper or in databases. Money, in a nutshell, is a social contract for which goods and services are exchanged. Until it gets converted back to its tangible or intangible form, it remains virtual. Sadly, many people cheat, steal, and even kill for a piece of this virtual reality.

Despite its stated value, the relative value of money can change dramatically based on your circumstances. A dollar that buys chilled water when you're dehydrated in a desert is priceless. If you were stranded on a desolate island next to a pot of gold, it would seem completely worthless. The gold would quickly become extremely valuable again if you could exchange it all for the opportunity to be rescued.

Some of the wealthiest people may be frustrated by personal loneliness, consumed by the search for a cure for a loved one's illness, or even vilified due to public disgrace. I imagine many of them would be willing to fork over a large chunk of money in order to reverse their circumstances.

My personal journey has taken me to some depths financially I never knew existed. I was not born with that proverbial silver spoon of privilege. I pretty much have earned every penny I've got. I've always had relatively conservative spending habits. That wasn't really the problem. Being a pauper more than a prince was what I was used to.

In the hopes of accelerating my personal wealth and savings, I made a few investments that turned out to be ill-advised nightmares. They were heavily weighted toward real estate just prior to the bust and recession. I was the poster boy for buying high and selling low. I went into debt to finance those ventures, and my net worth was literally wiped out. This took me to the brink of bankruptcy. I had to deal with lenders on various foreclosures and short sales.

I could have easily quit on myself, but I didn't, and I believe I ended up becoming stronger because of the difficult financial times I experienced. These events taught me how important economic well-being is as one of life's Core Assets. They sparked my desire to become financially smarter, hence my MBA. My missteps ultimately gave me a chance to become wiser through the school of hard knocks. I learned more about myself and what was truly important to me in life. Money can easily be taken away, but not once did I allow it to take away from my other Core Assets.

Before we get into the nitty-gritty of dealing with money in our lives, let me throw out a few names so you can tell me what immediately comes into your mind. Okay, let's begin.

What do you think of when you hear Michael Jackson? How about Bill Gates? Albert Einstein? Michael Jordan?

The answers I would expect to hear are King of Pop, Microsoft, theory of relativity, and basketball superstar. What you probably couldn't answer would be each individual's exact net worth. You probably didn't even really care. Well, that's the whole point. This is where the importance of money reaches its limit.

In life's grand scheme, a lot of things matter more than how much money you are able to amass in your lifetime. You may not be as well-known as the people I've mentioned here, but you, your family, your circle of friends, and all those around you will remember and appreciate how much your career, good deeds, and friendship have meant and made a difference in their lives. If you happen to be blessed with money, good for you. Don't feel guilty about it or fear it. Just remember that ultimately no one will remember you for how much you made; instead, you'll be remembered for what you did and how you impacted the people you encountered along the way. There is more than one way to make an impact in the world in order to live a satisfying and meaningful life.

It is true: money can't buy everything. As true as this statement may seem, it still comes with a big HOWEVER in that money can certainly make your life a bit easier. Since the existence of money is the reality we live in, why not accept it for what it is and what it isn't?

Without a doubt, everything has a cost. That means when it comes to each of our Core Assets, some things can and must be bought to improve our lives. Do you want to optimize your physical health? Medical care has a cost. A gym membership has a cost, as does any extra guidance you may need such as a personal trainer, exercise DVDs, or a yoga class. Eating healthy means preparing fresh foods. However, some of the healthiest ingredients in both procurement (organic) and preparation may turn out to be the most expensive. The less-healthy, preservative-filled foods are much cheaper. Even if you decide to check out a book from the library filled with recipes for your newly adopted raw foods diet, you still take on the indirect cost through your local taxes.

Your ROI on intellect will increase dramatically with a good education, which of course has its steep costs through tuition and public taxes. Even learning about something solely for personal enjoyment starts to add up. Whether you're into anything from gardening to astronomy, you'll need books, compost, star charts, an amateur telescope, heirloom seeds, or whatever other items support your hobby.

Dating is definitely not free. Counting your pennies while you're wining and dining won't make the best impression. Nobody likes a cheap date. Aside from courtship, what about traveling to a relative's wedding, meeting a friend for a movie, or planning a family dream vacation? That takes money. When you fly, there are fees bundled into your ticket to help support the FAA and TSA to keep you safe; again, more money.

There are costs associated with just about everything, especially for your overall wellness. We've mentioned food, but we haven't even looked at other basic living expenses like housing, phone, utilities, and day-to-day transportation. Many of us are fortunate enough to take these for granted, but it is important to think about the financial aspect that makes all of it possible. In our society, on various levels, we buy our security and means to survive. We pay into ways to be taken care of beyond our working years. So in this very real sense, although it may not buy everything, money does go a good distance toward buying much of our happiness.

GET A JOB

That old song "Get a Job," in a way, had the right idea. Because money will need to flow out of your pockets, you need a way to put some back in. But you don't need just any job. Many financial advisers will omit telling you this very important fact: your job or career is your number-one most important economic asset. This is where many of you will probably achieve the bulk of your positive cash flow. You owe it to yourself to give it your best effort. Once the cash is flowing, you can take care of your basic needs, save, and invest.

What are some of the common themes you hear when the people you know talk about their jobs? For most of us, "I can't stand my coworkers," "Waiting for five o'clock," or "TGIF" are the comments you are much more likely to hear instead of, "I love my job." That's a shame. With so many people only counting down the days until their next vacation, they spend vast energy feeding their own distaste for their jobs rather than working to optimize those forty-odd hours each week. That's nearly a third of some people's lives caught up in unhappiness. However, you should probably take it for granted that there are people lined up ready to take any job that you may have, especially in a tough economy.

Turning around those negative feelings can have not only an emotional benefit but a financial one as well. One of the most important factors that leads to flourishing in a job is **attitude**. I like to think of what Confucius said, "Choose a job you love, and you will never have to work a day in your life."

Whether through determination and a little luck you've found a deeply fulfilling career path, or if you're making the best of your current work situation, there is plenty to do to keep yourself engaged. Remember, it's not only getting a job that's important. You have to protect it.

A powerful way to think about the work you do is to envision ways you can be most effective on the job. What do you bring to the table that is unique? Think deeply about that question and you will recognize the strengths you have that will keep your work positive, focused, and relevant.

Here are some things you can do to stay in good graces on the job:

- **Be a team player**. Success is best achieved when everyone works together. Avoid the "me first" syndrome. Think of the well-being of everyone involved, and you will develop a winning attitude.

- **Be proactive**. If you notice a potential problem, don't rush to register a complaint. Try your best to be a problem solver rather than a problem creator. Your new idea may be the one to save the day. Don't ask what your company can do for you, but what you can do for your company.

- **Be calm**. Alarmism and negativity can spread easily to become a cancer in the organization. Instead take a deep breath and do your best to stay calm in trying times.

- **Be responsible and organized**. Answer your calls and email in a timely manner. Keep your work area organized and uncluttered. Remember to dot your i's and cross your t's—this attention to detail will get you noticed.

- **Be visible**. Don't be afraid to speak up and ask questions. These are valuable traits in an employee. Dressing to impress in a professional setting has many advantages. Don't be afraid to get to know your boss and your coworkers. If you would prefer to stay out of sight and fly under the radar, working on your assertiveness may help break this pattern. Invisible people are often the first to be let go.

- **Be friendly and approachable**. Tips from chapter 6 on relationships can come in handy here. Work on your communication so you can make suggestions and take criticism in the right spirit. Firm handshakes, eye contact, confidence, and active listening will all put you in good standing.

- **Be up to date**. Take advantage of continuing education opportunities and stay updated in your field. It doesn't take long to become a dinosaur. Remember, there is always someone out there waiting to replace you.

- **Be on your best behavior**. Don't get caught in scandals involving harassment, sexual abuse, substance abuse, or other ethical issues like stealing. Those are major-league problems that could haunt you for your entire career.

With all these pointers to focus on, when would you ever have time to fall into a pattern of complaint or to feel like a slave to your job? Instead take on those responsibilities and choose your positive outlook.

Your occupation will provide for you and your loved ones. Depending on what you choose, it may serve a societal or civic duty or be a way to carry on a family tradition. Your job might convey a sense of prestige and status and will virtually always be an opportunity for personal growth and fulfillment.

Your job performance is very important. Try to find what will make you happy and do your best once you're in that position. Your stability and income are the fundamental building blocks of all the other opportunities we examine in this chapter.

NEEDS, WANTS, AND WHIMS

I'm hopeful you have found your dream job, and you are generating all the money you need and more. The next step is to think about how you spend what you earn. Not all expenditures are created equal. It is important to take care of your needs first.

MANDATORY SPENDING

There are two main types of spending. The first is *mandatory spending*. This category is for the things you need to have for basic survival and for a reasonably secure means of living. Food and beverages, clothing, rental fees or mortgage, and transportation expenses are among the things you really need.

Mandatory spending doesn't end there. Now come the dreaded taxes. Yes, taxes can stir up a great deal of negativity. You might be asking yourself, "Why is the government taking away some of my hard-earned money?"

Most advanced nations have some form of taxation system in place. This becomes mandatory spending when the other alternative is jail time for evasion or stiff penalties for avoidance. Since taxes are not optional, you may as well look at the positives.

One of the most important aspects regarding tax expenditure is the ability to consolidate resources to create a collective benefit. In other words, taxes help make economies of scale possible. Public safety, for instance—everything from police, firefighters, air traffic control, national defense, consumer protection, drug safety, and more—is all paid for in part by public funding. It would be very expensive and nearly impossible for each individual to hire these services a la carte.

So even though most of us don't like paying them, our taxes do go toward things that make all of our lives better. However, efficient spending of taxes seems to be a chronic challenge no matter what side of the political fence you are on. While each political side rages on about how the other's view on spending is wasteful, I prefer to work with what we have and leave the debate for the politicos.

The tax code is very complex and always changing. The IRS doesn't necessarily make it easy to understand even for professional CPAs, let alone the layperson. However, a tax professional like a CPA is equipped to keep on top of all the current regulations and is there to help you when you need it. Software packages are also available if your tax return is fairly simple.

Don't be afraid to seek advice and take advantage of whatever tax breaks the code will offer you. Finding those savings may actually give you a higher ROI than stock market investments. It is well worth the time and effort. If you end up receiving a tax refund, congratulations! You just loaned that money to the government interest free for an entire year. If you end up paying taxes, congratulations again! You were able to make some money over the past year.

Savings also fall under mandatory spending. Even though you will not technically be spending it, you will be allocating it away. Saving is important because it allows you to fund your own personal self-insurance and to keep your financial boat afloat. How much do you need to save? Ideally you should create a personal self-insurance (emergency) fund that could finance your needs for three to six months. Unexpected events can and do happen. As secure as we all like to feel from day to day, you never know when your company will decide to downsize, your landlord will give you notice that she's selling the property, or your car will strand you in the middle of rush hour. It is best to be prepared for life's changes.

Aside from this emergency fund, your savings should also encompass long-range goals like investing in a retirement plan and college funds. These include various ERISA-qualified IRAs (Roth, SEP, SIMPLE), pensions, and college 529 plans, among others. With the power of compound interest, you can really grow your savings exponentially over the long haul. The earlier you start saving, the better your returns and your preparation for the future.

DISCRETIONARY SPENDING

Well, that might sound like a whole lot of money locked up under mandatory spending. You may be asking, "When do I get to have any fun with my hard-earned cash?" Allowing your money to help you enjoy life is important, too. This is called *discretionary spending*. Do you like to splurge on dinner with friends? How about taking the whole family out to see the latest Hollywood action flick? Thinking about taking that tour of London and Liverpool you've always dreamed about? Maybe you'd finally like to buy the completely impractical but gorgeous party outfit you keep eyeing in the city. After you've taken care of all the necessities, go ahead and splurge on your wants and whims.

Think of your discretionary spending as paying yourself. You certainly deserve it. Make sure, though, to avoid borrowing to do it. Paying yourself knowing that all the important things are in order is satisfying, especially knowing that you haven't borrowed your lifestyle but earned it.

Learning to spend responsibly and sticking to the plan may present difficulties for a lot of us. Try not to beat yourself up if money problems have been in your history. This is your chance to turn it around and get on the right track. The first step to that is getting a handle on what can go wrong:

- **Societal pressures** cause a lot of problems with spending. When it's all about keeping up with the Joneses, you'll wind up trying to impress with cars, clothes, and country clubs when the wealth for those things is not within your grasp.

- **Poor financial decision making** can be a wide-ranging problem. Unsound investment advice, not buying enough or the right kinds of insurance, overusing credit, leasing instead of buying, and impulsive spending can come together to create a sticky web of debt.

- **Ignoring the budget** once you've made it will not help you reach your goals. Budgets are very much like New Year's resolutions in that both tend to fade slowly out in time if no one is around to crack the whip. Sometimes, without immediate accountability like a school paper due on Monday morning, it is easy to become lax. Working with a family member, a good adviser, a business coach, or just a big dose of plain old determination may help you get back on track.

- **Credit cards**, when overused, can easily become the bane of your existence. The more you charge, the more the fees add up, making it hard to keep up and pay it off. High interest rates are often among the most profitable aspects of a bank's business. When you go to use credit, think about whether it is a short-term loan for something necessary, or if you will wind up stuffing a bank's coffers for something that will only give you temporary satisfaction.

- **Addictions**, on a whole lot of levels, can do you in. The price paid in loss of physical and mental health can be beyond measure. Speaking in financial terms, regular use of cigarettes, drugs, and alcohol becomes incredibly costly. A pack of cigarettes a day at seven to eight dollars each over twenty to thirty years easily adds up to more than a million dollars over a lifetime. Life-affirming, healthy activities will not only help keep you safe from these demons, but can also surely save you a lot of money.

So let's raise the ROI on your spending. There are a lot of good things to do and healthy habits to develop. Try these:

- **Pay your bills on time**. Avoid those unnecessary fees. If it suits your situation, set up AutoPay so as not to be late.

- **Learn when to borrow**. Get a handle on your spending by deciding what constitutes a reason to borrow. Borrowing for something that will serve you for a long time—like a home or your education—makes sense. Using credit cards to fund an expensive vacation when you are already in debt does not. If you must borrow, it's usually best to do so for an asset that will increase in value rather than decrease.

- **Pay with cash**. If credit card spending has been a problem for you, try keeping cash in your pocket instead. Sometimes seeing how much something costs in actual paper money will act as a deterrent. It is a lot easier to charge a hundred bucks that you never really see than to watch a hundred-dollar bill slip from your hands.

- **Go for bargains**. It is more than okay to opt for the less expensive items. Generic brands are often just fine; many are even name brands repackaged. Buying used and refurbished things can be virtually good as new. Try fixing something that is broken before automatically spending money on a replacement. Take bargain shopping for the adventure it can be. Even the wealthy like to do it. Remember, it is never a bargain if you really can't afford it. Keep your discretion and common sense engaged.

- **Make saving for future plans work for you**. Get in on tax-advantaged retirement accounts if you can. If your employer can match your savings, that's a big bonus. Look for a tax-advantaged college savings plan. Encourage great academic performance that might result in a scholarship. Keep your eyes open for other similar savings opportunities. To start thinking about growing your money for the future through investment, try the Rule of 72 in the CAPS at the end of this chapter.

- **Ask questions**. Before buying, remember to ask yourself:
  "Do I really need it?"
  "Can I do without it?"
  "What are some alternatives?"
  Get in the habit of taking the time to reflect, and you will be much more likely to make wiser choices.

THE SPECTER OF DEBT

Sometimes big things come up and you need to borrow money. It may be time for you to go back to school or buy a home. It may be time for you to take a chance on a new business. You might simply find yourself in lean times and have to make ends meet. Whatever the reason, it is not uncommon for most of us, at some point, to have to deal with debt.

Debt can be classified into several forms. The most common is consumer debt, which may include credit card debt, payday loans, overdrafts, and personal loans. These debts are considered unsecured because there is no collateral to back the loans. Interest rates tend to be higher since unsecured debt is riskier for the lender.

Secured debt is so called because there is collateral involved. The lender makes the loan so the borrower can buy something big, like a house or a car. If the loan is not paid, the borrower will eventually be forced to forfeit the collateral. Since risk is lowered for the lender by the attached collateral, interest rates tend to be a bit lower. Consumer and business debt can fall into the secured debt category. Examples include a mortgage, a home equity loan, an auto loan, or a business loan.

A lender might cast himself as your best friend at the beginning of a deal, but when things go sour he can quickly become your worst nightmare. The best advice when it comes to a secured loan is this: don't mess up. Make sure you are ready to take on that mortgage or car loan before you make the jump.

Unsecured consumer debt, left unchecked, is a runaway problem. Again there are legitimate reasons to use credit cards from time to time. They can also be used problematically to keep up an illusion of wealth, power, and unlimited funds. If you wake up one day and find you've gotten into considerable debt in this way, try to find a way to begin paying off your credit cards consistently and as quickly as possible. The consequences of unpaid, unsecured debt can start out with missed payment penalties and calls from collection agencies and move right up into liens against properties, garnished wages, and account seizures.

You may hear some financial advisers talking about *good debt* and *bad debt*. According to some, investing in a home is good debt because you get to realize the mortgage interest tax breaks and other related tax breaks from the interest of the debt. This type of advice recommends paying off the debt slowly. The money you would otherwise use to pay down the debt is then freed up for investments that will yield high returns. These advisers maintain that there is an opportunity cost to paying off that debt, namely the loss of a chance at those tax breaks and higher returns. Some disciplined investors can make money this way.

Call me cynical, but I see a conflict of interest in advice like this as it pertains to most people. It stands to reason to me that the sooner you are debt free, the sooner you achieve a better financial situation and greater peace of mind. But what if the bulk of your money was used to pay down debt? That would result in much less money available for the commissions of advisers, stockbrokers, insurance agents, and so on.

My advice for maximum financial ROI is to be proactive about paying off your debts. Rather than waiting until near retirement to pay off your home, think about what it would be like to be finished ten or even twenty years earlier. If affording your own home is not within immediate reach, consider renting as a viable option. By renting, you avoid mortgage interest and insurance, property taxes, home insurance, and maintenance costs, and you can take what would have been a 20 percent down payment and invest it elsewhere. Plus, you don't have a creditor to deal with, which isn't a bad thing after all.

Remember, it is very easy to be overly optimistic about your circumstances and to borrow money based on that feeling. All too often borrowers find out that it is a lot easier to borrow money than it is to pay it back. To get out of debt, take the time to put your priorities in order. Pay for your bare necessities while paying down the debt as diligently as you can. You may miss that dinner-and-a-movie night, the newest electronic gadgets, and expensive weekend getaways for a little while, but putting discretionary spending on ice while you dig your way out of trouble is well worth the temporary shift in lifestyle.

It would be nice if we lived in an ideal world and we could all pay for our assets outright. We would live in a state of financial freedom. Barring that, secured debt can help you make the large purchases when you need to. Credit cards, when paid in full each month, are fine, but overall keep in mind that debt is not your friend. As we've seen in recent world events in Greece and Spain, too much debt can bring even sovereign nations to their knees.

INVESTING: TAKING THE CALCULATED RISK

Once you determine that your income is steady, your spending is in balance, and your debt is under control, it is a good time to start thinking about investing. Prior to making the leap, you may be introduced to something called a *risk tolerance test*, a questionnaire used to figure out what kind of investor you will be. I find the name of this test to be a bit of a misnomer, and a very telling one. Why not call it a *benefit tolerance test*? You do stand to gain money, just as you may lose money with investments. Must we always see the glass half empty? Maybe there is good reason for this, and it's best not to sugarcoat it.

Let's take a look at some of the risks you may encounter when investing. First there is capital risk. This is the money you put up to invest. You may lose some or all of your capital. Next is liquidity risk. How easily can that investment be sold, or liquidated? Stocks, for example, are generally more liquid than real estate. In some economic climates, it can be very difficult to unload an illiquid asset.

Then there is interest rate risk—meaning the value of your investments may fluctuate based on the underlying interest rate. There is also credit risk. For instance, if you buy bonds and the issuer defaults, your investment will lose value. Because exchange rates change all the time, if you buy or sell across foreign markets, there is currency risk. Current events can always change the markets, so there is an additional risk there.

It is quite true that you can lose money through investing. Understand that money is a lot easier to lose than it is to earn. Once lost, it takes more effort to get it back. For every 10 percent lost, it takes 11 percent in earnings to regain the original amount. If there is a 20 percent loss, you'll need to earn 25 percent back. Sustaining a 40 percent loss means you need a 67 percent return just to get back to even. A 50 percent loss means you need to stage a 100 percent comeback to be back to square one.

So, as ace investor Warren Buffett once said, "If at all possible, don't lose money." Now you can see why advisers are not so worried about your ability to accept gains—your benefit tolerance—as your ability to tolerate risk, vis-à-vis losing money. Hence the name *risk tolerance test*.

Still reading? I didn't mean to scare you off. I advocate investing, albeit wise investing. Just be sure you enter into it with your eyes wide open. A disciplined approach will likely yield the greatest chance of success. You may consider yourself an aggressive, a moderate, or a conservative investor. No matter what label you choose, it is important to be aware of the inherent risks.

Because of all the possible risks, a lot of people think of investing as a form of gambling. If you're investing for the long term, that is not usually the case. However it may be a truer statement if you are speculating. This is the practice of attempting to profit from short-term fluctuations in the market by guessing which way a stock or other asset will go. When you speculate, you place bets on the market almost as if it is a casino. Similar to sports gambling, information is used from various sources to make an educated bet. Insiders have more information while most regular folks get information far too late to react. The regular guy sitting at his or her home computer in his PJs, trying to outsmart the market, has no idea that he is up against multibillion-dollar investment firms with unlimited resources invested in supercomputer-automated trading algorithms and teams of MBAs. To call it a David and Goliath situation doesn't come close.

These poor day traders are like schools of minnows in waters filled with institutional sharks. For every winner there is usually a loser. Guess who is usually the loser?

Institutions tend to buy low and sell high. Retail investors, working from limited knowledge and information, often wind up buying high and selling low. Greed and fear are often the retail investor's primary psychological drivers. Unfortunately they aren't very good drivers. The key is to make your investments as little like gambling as possible. Forget speculating, and make your investing a disciplined, long-term proposition.

One feature of wise investing is diversification. For example, many people choose mutual funds, which are spread out across many companies and industries, in order to gain broad exposure to the markets. This offsets some of the risks in their portfolio. The funds are usually held for long periods to maximize being in the market during the days of greatest profit.

Though mutual funds are still very popular, I'd like to make another suggestion—low-cost index funds. These funds, collectively called *exchange-traded funds* or ETFs, are instruments that are traded on the stock exchange and are treated much like stocks. They can track various market indices such as the S&P, Dow, NASDAQ, and Russell. ETFs are relatively inexpensive and tax efficient. They cover a broad spectrum of the market, so your diversification is built right in. They are very transparent—they can be priced in real time while mutual funds are priced at day's end. Unlike actively managed funds, ETFs are not dependent on any particular manager, so you are not beholden to a revolving door or personnel change.

Most advisers use the S&P 500 as a benchmark for investment performance. However, very few actually beat the market. Up to 90 percent of actively managed funds fail to beat the S&P on a consistent, long-term basis. That being said, if you can't beat it, why not join it?

Dollar cost averaging is a method that might be helpful to you as you work your way into investing. This is the practice of putting a consistent amount of money into the market per given period, usually on a monthly basis. This way you can generate funds for investment in smaller increments, buy fewer shares when stocks are higher, and buy more when they are cheaper. However, if you have the money to do it in one shot, investing with a lump sum may work even better over the long term.

Here are several other kinds of investments you may decide to make, along with their plusses and minuses (please note that you should seek proper financial advice where indicated):

- **Stocks** can prove to be good protectors against inflation over the long term. Their risks are volatility and, of course, the fact that there are no guarantees.

- **Options** are derivatives of stocks and other assets such as commodities in which you can purchase the right to buy or sell a certain number of stocks, typically in blocks of 100 shares. The risk in options lies in their deterioration over time, when they ultimately expire as worthless.

- **Bonds** can guarantee their principal value when held to their maturity date. They offer consistent regular payments over their life spans. Because of their decreased risk, they can give you some peace of mind. Value will fluctuate, though, with changes in inflation and underlying interest rates. As interest rates go up, bond valuation will go down.

It is important to pay attention to bond ratings: In the event that a bond issuer defaults, bonds may become significantly devalued or worthless. Junk bonds may pay more since they have lower ratings and a higher risk of default.

- **Real estate** can provide good inflation protection. However, it can make for a problematic investment in a poor economy, especially when it's heavily leveraged with financing. Real estate investments tend to be illiquid assets and are therefore harder to sell. But they do offer many tax advantages. These include deductions in depreciation, interest expenses, and real property taxes.

- **Collectibles** can be great fun if you enjoy them. If you find the right buyer for your type of items, everyone can walk away happy. However, investing in things such as coins, artwork, watches, jewelry, or other items means your assets may be illiquid. There are no guarantees as to the genuine nature or condition of your collectibles, and keeping them stored may prove difficult or costly.

Things to keep in mind:

- **Don't get emotional**. When markets soar, greed can set in, and when markets tank, fear can set in. Both scenarios can easily lead to economic disaster. Avoid panic selling, joining the herd, overmonitoring, overtrading, and overattachment to the investment asset or fund.

- **Don't try to game the system**. Really. By timing the market, you can actually miss out on the most important days. Between 1996 and 2006, there was an overall 9.4 percent return. If you take away the ten most important days, your return would be only 2 percent. You may get lucky timing the market a few times on a short-term basis, but over the long haul it's a losing proposition. Market timing simply doesn't work. Just ask the casinos why they love gamblers when they play for long periods of time. By timing their bets over the long haul, you will most likely walk out with empty pockets. Happy casinos, happy Wall Street.

- **Don't rely on friends and family for investment tips**. Your broker, your adviser, and your own knowledge of your financial situation should carry more weight than hearsay.

- **Don't get suckered by a sales pitch in a phone call or email**. If you feel pressured by a sales pitch from anyone at all, ignore it and run away. Due diligence is very important; there is no need for quick decisions. Don't be afraid to ask them to prove their claims by showing you actual brokerage statements, audited financial statements, and tax returns. I doubt you will ever get any of them. Remember, if it sounds too good to be true, it probably is.

KEEPING WHAT YOU HAVE: YOUR FINANCIAL SAFETY

You may already have a job you love to go to every day, or you may still be looking for greater fulfillment and stability. Maybe you've just saved up enough and think you're ready to plan your first big vacation. Do you have a good, diversified portfolio yet, or are you still hoping to pay off a credit card before looking into investments?

Wherever you are on your financial journey, it is essential that you look out for what you already have. The very best advice for asset protection is simple, but it extends into many aspects of life: make good decisions, and stay out of trouble.

That might sound like the blanket advice Mom and Dad used to dish out, but this is the advanced version, aimed specifically at not allowing you and your money to be so easily parted. Your solutions? Let's start out with good insurance and good behavior.

So many adversities can happen—unexpected general expenses, medical costs, wild weather events, you just never know. Sudden, unplanned losses are major causes of bankruptcy. A strong shield against this is proper insurance.

There are so many types of insurance that I couldn't list them all. Homeowner's or renter's insurance will protect your home and the things in it. Doctors, pharmacists, and many others need professional liability insurance. Disability insurance will protect your number-one financial asset—your cash flow—during your active working years. Term life insurance will protect your loved ones in the event of your untimely death.

Long-term care insurance also has its role in protecting your wealth if you are incapacitated later in life. Umbrella insurance is valuable in protecting against lawsuits from injuries and other events. Businesses typically need to carry general liability insurance, errors and omissions insurance, and director and officers insurance.

As you can see, there is a broad spectrum of insurance needs. On the behavior end, it's all about using good ol' common sense. It's very much like deciding to walk alone into a dark alley—it's a poor decision, and you're asking for trouble. So stay out of the dark alleys of life: Avoid questionable or fraudulent transactions. Don't drink and drive. Get enough sleep if your work requires full concentration or quick reflexes. Take care of your property and eliminate problems, like dead trees or broken sidewalks that could cause injury. Divorces are financially and psychologically painful, so do pay attention to your relationships. Avoid becoming a guarantor for someone else on a loan. Always read the fine print on anything you sign.

Look at the bottom line. A wrong turn in any of these scenarios can not only hurt you and others; it can also wind up costing you a whole lot of money in the end. If for that reason alone, proceed with caution.

Here are some other asset protection steps you can take:

- **Be aware of your state laws**. Some states are debtor-friendly while others are more lender-friendly. Make a wise decision before taking on any form of major debt.

- **Consider cash-value life insurance**. This type of insurance has a role in asset protection in that it can be far less expensive and more transparent than other fancier asset protection strategies. The general consensus is to buy term insurance and invest the rest. However from an asset protection standpoint, cash-value life insurance can be extremely valuable.

- **Take a separate loan**. If you are married, there is something to be said for keeping a good deal of the finances separate. If one person takes out a loan, it is beneficial to keep the other completely removed from the debt obligation as a guarantor. Co-ownership is still possible, especially in terms of a home. In some states a home deeded to a married couple (Tenancy by the Entirety) is protected from creditors so long as they remain a couple and there is only one person liable.

- **Consider ERISA-qualified retirement plans**. These are based on the Employee Retirement Income Security Act of 1974 and are not only great retirement tools, but are also great for asset protection. Creditors generally can't go after funds in a qualified retirement plan even in bankruptcy.

- **Form a legal entity**. When you form an LLC or C corporation, significant financial protections will follow, provided you maintain strict compliance. Among many stipulations, personal and business transactions cannot be mixed. Seek proper legal advice when going this route.

- **Form a trust**. Trusts are legal agreements by which a person or entity entrusts another to hold assets for a third party. These are seen at work for charitable purposes and for will and estate planning, and are commonly used in pension plans. There are many different kinds of trusts out there. One size does not fit all. There is a children's trust, credit shelter trust, dynasty trust, irrevocable and inalienable trust, charitable remainder trust, personal residence trust, and foreign trust, just to name a few.

- **Get your affairs in order early**. Don't wait to draw up a will or power of attorney. Revocable trusts may be useful to avoid probate. Once again, proper legal advice specific to your state law is the best way to go.

One thing to keep in mind is that these asset-protection strategies only work when you are not in any sort of current trouble or state of liability. Once you attempt to try to protect yourself while you are in trouble, it's simply too late. It's considered fraudulent transfer when you try to hide or give away assets when an adverse event has occurred or is imminent. Anything you do will become null and void, and most likely will be reversed if this is found to be the case. Therefore don't wait for something bad to happen. Be proactive and start protecting yourself long before any unforeseen event occurs.

Now that we've considered some strategies that can help you hold on to your money, let's look at how letting go of some of it can be of benefit, too.

GIVING BACK VIA CHARITY

No matter what amount of money you earn in your lifetime, your philosophy, your culture, your affinities or differences, everyone is here on this planet together. Ultimately it isn't all about looking out for number one. In our search to do the best for ourselves, we should never forget the importance of charity.

Here we'll look at five main types of charity. The level of personal giving increases with each category. You'll notice that a nice bonus effect of charity is that it often works like instant karma—the good kind. I have come up with a classification of charities that gives a bit more clarification on the subject:

- **Indirect charity** is actually simply taking care of yourself. By taking care of yourself, you're not only doing yourself a favor, but you're doing society a favor. Strange as that may sound, it is quite true. By living safely you don't endanger others. By being financially responsible, you are doing your part to keep the whole economy stable. Get a good

education and you contribute with your work, your awareness, and your potential. Care enough for yourself to maximize all of your Core Assets and you will already be making
a big contribution.

- **Passive charity** is writing a check to a favorite charitable
organization or donating used items. This is as simple as
taking the time to give away the things you decide to get
rid of during spring cleaning or giving a positive response
to that annual fund-raising call. This is one of the most
common forms of charity. You'll be giving up a nominal
financial asset and will gain a small tax deduction along
the way.

- **Sponsorship** is primarily for businesses that sponsor
events for charitable purposes. Charities are usually thrilled
to land sponsorships from major corporations. The corporations, in return, get great marketing tools and great ROI
for brand awareness. It's a win-win situation.

- **Active charity** is volunteerism, plain and simple. In this
case you not only help generate funds for a charity but also
give up some of your personal time. You may participate
in a silent auction, a charity ball, a walk-a-thon, or some
other event for a good cause. For your effort you may find
great networking opportunities, take part in a healthy
activity, receive prestige, and have a lot of fun along the
way.

- **Ultimate charity** is charity with no strings attached. In
other words there are no tax breaks, no publicity or media
attention, no accolades, or any other of the usual perks.
It is charity in which you might make a large anonymous

financial donation, or perhaps travel to a third-world country, spending personal funds and possibly even putting yourself at risk to perform an important service for others in need. I recommend having the experience of doing some ultimate charity at least once in your life. Your ROI will still be there in the form of lifelong memories and personal fulfillment.

- **Charitable remainder trusts (CRTs)** offer an opportunity for more financially savvy businesses or high net worth individuals who want to perform charity on a larger scale. You might consider setting up a CRT to benefit the charity of your choice along with your own financial and estate planning.

- **Charitable foundations** can allow you to do some of the same things a CRT does, but with more control over income and with a potentially reduced estate tax.

- **Nonprofit charitable corporations** are tax-exempt charities with certain restrictions and compliance requirements. Extra funds cannot be used for private interests, but this type of corporation can provide a means to support family members in future generations if they serve as corporate officers, trustees, or directors.

- **Donor-advised funds** are good for people with lower incomes. Overseen by major mutual funds, contributions can grow tax-free and are tax deductible.

Giving is a very satisfying thing. It doesn't have to be financial. Giving through any and all of these methods not only makes the world a better place, but also brightens your own spirit and sense of well-being. No matter how big or how small the charities I've helped, the experiences have all been memorable. The joy and happiness I've seen on the faces of those who have received something they desperately needed will always remain with me. There is something especially wonderful about friends made through volunteering while discovering goodwill and gratitude on all sides of the equation. As I said, making money might drive a lot in this world, but when you're met with a genuine smile, it's clear money isn't everything.

CAPS FOR ROI ON ECONOMIC HEALTH

Incorporate these **C**ORE **A**SSET **P**ROTECTION **S**TRATEGIES and new tips into your money-related habits to strengthen your economic health.

1. **Appreciate what you have.** It's a lot easier to lose money than to make it. This makes it even more important that you take care of what you've spent your precious time and energy earning. Employ all the knowledge, resources, and will you can muster to hold on to your nest egg and help it grow.

2. **Think before you buy.** Avoid impulse purchases and spending sprees by slowing down and asking questions: Do I really need this item or do I just want it? Do I want to buy it simply because it seems like a great deal? Can I live without it? What might I consider instead? Remember, you'll never miss that frivolous item if you never had it to begin with.

3. **Be frugal, not cheap.** Don't worry about a stigma of being frugal. It just means you spend wisely and that you seek the best value in the things you buy. Being cheap means you're out for the lowest price no matter what. Your overall ROI will be higher when you weigh your options with frugality.

4. **Take care of yourself during lean times.** If ever you find yourself dealing with financial stress for any reason, focus on maintaining health in the other Core Assets while you work to fix the money problem. Left unrecognized, the loss of a job or another financial stressor can lead to mental strain and depression, relationship troubles, shaken spiritual faith, and even physical shifts like a lack of will to exercise. Make extra efforts to nurture connections with loved ones, practice your spirituality, be social, and keep your body healthy. Stay in balance and you're more likely to be back on your feet in no time.

5. **Out of work?** Work on improving. While between jobs, take steps to become more employable and essential while maintaining overall balance. Watch your spending and avoid unsecured debt. Be careful not to take out frustrations on your personal relationships. Do some introspective analysis: How is my work performance—Careless? Detailed? Cheerful? Begrudging? Think about those in your field who inspire you, and study what makes them successful. Use the downtime for extra education and training. People in the workforce appreciate expertise and diversity. Make sure you're ready when it's time to jump.

6. **Try the Rule of 72.** Here is a simple way to think about how your money can grow through investment. The Rule of 72 is used to calculate compound interest. Divide 72 by the interest rate per year, and that will tell you how many years it will take for your money to double. You can use the same basic formula to calculate the interest rate it will take to double your money within a given period. The earlier you invest, the more compound interest will be of benefit to you.

7. **You can't miss something you never had.** There is more pain in losing money than in the joy of gaining it. Why? Once something is experienced, the feeling of it is known and remembered. It becomes harder to let go. A million dollars will never be missed if you never earned it to begin with. Perhaps that's why many cultures and societies appear happy with so little. They don't know what that kind of wealth is like.

   However, people who have had it will sorely miss it once it's lost. This is why bankruptcy is considered more of a major, life-changing event than winning the lottery. It ranks right up there with marriage, death, job loss, and sickness.

8. **Keep it in perspective.** No matter how much you strive for financial gain, it is best to remember that we enter the world with nothing, and we eventually leave with nothing. Most of us would trade everything material for freedom, friends, and intimacy. It would mean nothing to be sitting on top of piles of gold and silver if you were the only person on earth. So allow money to help you satisfy some of your needs and wants. Enjoy it, but don't obsess. After all, as far as I know, you can't do a balance transfer to a bank account in the afterlife.

8

How God Is Good:
Your ROI on Spirituality

GROWING INTO (AND OUT OF) RELIGION

A young girl gives a recitation for the first time in front of her congregation on the occasion of her bat mitzvah. A man offers handshakes to those around him during a Sunday morning church service and feels goodwill among his friends, peers, and fellow worshippers. A boy goes camping far away from his home in the city, and as he stares up into the vast, starry sky, he gets his first profound sense of being part of an awe-inspiring universe.

These are just a few examples of experiences where spirituality plays an important role. No matter the specific religion or the absence of it, most of us at some point have a sense of some essence larger than ourselves. Spiritual experiences can do good work in our lives, so it is worth the time to consider maximizing your ROI on spirituality.

When naming this Core Asset, I chose the word spirituality because of its broad definition. For the purposes of this discussion, spirituality may be understood as spirituality and religion, if the latter is not named specifically. Explorations, experiences, and beliefs in these related, often very closely aligned arenas have great ROI potential, although they also have their cautionary tales. Let's consider a few good, working definitions for spirituality and religion to keep in mind as we move forward.

Spirituality may be thought of as anything that is concerned with the depth, meaning, and purpose of life. It is the exploration into thoughts or practices that provide feelings of connectedness among people, sometimes among people and all living things, and very often between people and the greater universe. A spiritual model may or may not include the concept of a supreme being.

Religion, on the other hand, tends to signify a more ordered and socialized set of practices. It is a language of behaviors, tenets, cultural expectations, and worship practices. Religions typically are centered on a form or forms of deity, spiritual leaders, and sacred texts. Ideally a religion is a pathway for accessing a sense of spirituality, although it is possible to have religiosity without spirituality. A growing number of people currently report being spiritual but not religious. Whatever the balance for any given individual, these practices have their benefits.

I was exposed to the concepts of religion at a very early age. I grew up in a family that held moderate Eastern values and beliefs.

In keeping with those values, we were primarily vegetarian. The idea of God felt natural and relatively easy to grasp when I was young because this was the worldview I heard being talked about all around me.

Not only did thinking about God give me the sense that I was loved and protected, but it also piqued my curiosity. Mischievous kid that I was, sometimes, out on the playground, I'd test out what it might be like if I were a supreme being. This wasn't always a good thing for the critters and bugs. Sometimes I'd just observe for long periods as ant colonies went about the business of their ordered chaos. Occasionally I'd throw out small bread crumbs, fascinated by how the ants would swarm, break down, and haul away treats much larger than I'd think they could carry. Sometimes the naughty side of me would take over and I'd pour water on them, unleashing the wrath of God and observing their struggles. If I was in a really bad mood, their fate would be handed down with a can of Raid.

I guess I was beginning to grapple with understanding one of life's big mysteries, but I clearly hadn't yet contemplated the differences between red and black ants. It only took one time of toying with the stinging red ones for me to get a taste of my own medicine. I wasn't so quick to play God after that. It may not have been the kindest or most sophisticated way to think of divine power, but those times represent some of my early musings on the topic.

Once I began middle school, my spiritual education expanded. The public school I had been attending just wasn't living up to a standard that seemed acceptable. Even at my young age, I was sensitive to the fact that I was receiving a poor education. Drugs and smoking were commonplace in this particular public school. Teachers spent more time keeping kids in line than teaching—when they weren't on strike, that is. Eventually it became normal that I'd come home in the afternoon and tell Mom and Dad that school just wasn't an easy place to learn. The revelation led to my being enrolled in a nearby parochial school for the next six years.

Getting used to a new school isn't easy for most kids, and the element of religion was definitely an added puzzle for me to piece together. I'd heard about the Bible but had had very little exposure to it. And there I was in a school where we all took daily religion classes in a tradition quite different from the one in which I had been raised. At first I felt pretty awkward, but eventually I came to know more about Christianity than I knew about the religion into which I had been born.

This composite of home practices, class study, and tidbits I picked up along the way remained my main source of information on religion and spirituality throughout high school. In college I absorbed even more. The demographics around me widened, and suddenly I was meeting people with quite a spectrum of beliefs. Up until that point in my life, I hadn't met many people who followed Judaism, Buddhism, or Islam. I also came in contact with those who pursued lesser-known paths, and those who considered themselves spiritual without the aid of a particularly defined, historical religious path. I never felt prejudice or uneasiness about any of them. I found the array of belief systems interesting, and I saw the positive benefits those beliefs seemed to bring to those who followed them.

Then came a day that changed everything: September 11, 2001.

I was living in the Washington, DC, area on the morning of those infamous attacks on the United States. In fact, I lived little more than two miles from the Pentagon when it was attacked. The plumes of smoke emanating from the fortress formed a lasting memory for me, along with the chaos from the lockdowns and curfews. News spread of suicide bombers and planes used as weapons in New York, DC, and Pennsylvania, as did the waves of shock, grief, outrage, confusion, and fear. As the country and the world were affected on the macrocosmic scale, my personal landscape underwent its own seismic shift: my outlook took a sudden turn, and religion suddenly looked and felt like danger dressed in fancy robes.

Because the 9/11 attacks were attributed to religious extremists, this terrible tragedy led me to take a good look at religion's dark side. I saw the counterhatred, profiling, and outright prejudice that sprang up in response to the attacks. The terrible realities of the Crusades in the Middle Ages, the Spanish Inquisition, and the Holocaust, which still lives in recent historical memory, sprang to my mind. I lost my faith in religion then, disgusted by the way these staunch and dueling beliefs seemed to be at the center of all our worst wars and human persecutions. I gave up being a vegetarian and the other tenets with which I'd been raised, and most of those I'd embraced along the way.

My life became quite secular, although I never consciously gave up on faith. I still had half an eye on spiritual and religious matters, but it is fair to say I stopped giving them much thought. I was happy to move away from the religious storylines that seemed to cause so much pain. This would change again for me, but not before a good deal of time and further contemplation.

THE BATTLES FOR BELIEFS

There are an estimated 7 billion people today who call planet earth home. Many of those people claim religious faith as part of their lives. There are 2.1 billion Christians; 1.5 billion people who follow Islam; 900 million who practice Hinduism; 376 million are

Buddhists; 394 million follow the Chinese traditional religion; and 14 million practice Judaism (www.adherents.com).

This is only the tip of the iceberg. Take a look at the following list of world religions, both old and new. This vast diversity at first fueled my skepticism. With all of these varying beliefs, a good many of these people, I reasoned, must believe they are the only group with the answers. Could that be right?

Abenaki mythology
ACIM (A Course In Miracles)
Advaita Vedanta
African religions
Ahl-e Haqq (Yarsan)
Ahmadiyya
Akamba mythology
Akan mythology
Alawites
Alchemy
Aleut mythology
Alexandrian Wicca
Amish
Anabaptists
Ancient Mystical Order Rosae
    Crucis
Anglican Communion
Anglicanism
Anglo-Saxon mythology
Arès Pilgrim Movement
Asatru
Ashanti mythology
Assyrian Church of the East
Aum Shinrikyo (now known as
    Aleph)
Australian Aboriginal mythology
Aztec mythology
Bahá'í Faith
Baptists
Basque mythology
Blackfoot mythology
Buddhism
Bushongo mythology
Candomblé
Cao Dai
Cargo cults (John Frum, etc.)

Catholicism
Chippewa mythology
Christadelphians
Christianity
Christian mysticism
Christian new religious
    movements
Chukchi mythology
Church of England
Church of Ireland
The Church of Jesus Christ of
    Latter Day Saints (a.k.a. LDS)
Community of Christ
Confraternity of the Rose Cross
Confucianism
Conservative Judaism
Coptic Orthodox Church
Creativity Movement
Creek mythology
Creole religions
Crow mythology
Dahomey mythology
Dev Samaj
Dianic Wicca
Dievturiba
Dinka mythology
Druidry
Druze
Eastern Catholic Churches
Eastern Orthodoxy
Eclectic unification religions
Efik mythology
Egyptian mythology
Episcopal Church (United States)
Esotericism
Essenes

European religions
Evenk mythology
Faery Wicca
Faiths of indigenous peoples
Falasha Judaism
Falun Dafa (Falun Gong)
Feri Tradition
Finnish mythology
Finnish neopaganism
Freemasonry
Fundamentalist Church of Jesus
    Christ of Latter Day Saints (a.k.a.
    FLDS)
Gardnerian Wicca
Gaudiya Vaishnavism
Gnosticism
Greek Orthodox Church
Greek religion
Guarani mythology
Haida mythology
Haitian Voudun
Hanafi
Hanbali
Happy Science
Hasidic Judaism
Hawaiian religion
Hebrews
Helenism
Hellênismos
Hinduism
Hindu mysticism
Hindu philosophy
Humanism
Huron mythology
Hutterites
Ibadi
Ibo mythology
Iglesia ni Cristo
Inuit mythology
Iroquois mythology
ISKCON (Hare Krishna)
Islam
Ismaili
Isoko mythology
Jainism
Jehovah's Witnesses
Juche

Judaism
Judeo-Paganism
Kabbalah
Kagyupa
Kalam
Karaite Judaism
Kharijite
Khoikhoi mythology
Kwakiutl mythology
Lakota mythology
Latter Day Saint movement
    (Mormonism)
Law of One
Left-Hand Path religions
Lenape mythology
Lotuko mythology
Lugbara mythology
Lutheranism
Macumba
Mahayana
Maliki
Mandaeism
Manichaeism
Maori mythology
Martinism
Matrixism: The path of the One
Mennonites
Messianic Judaism
Methodism
Micronesian mythology
Middle Eastern religions
Modekngei (Republic of Palau)
Mohism
Muslim
Mysticism
Mytraism
Nation of Islam
Native American religions
Nauruan indigenous religion
Navaho mythology
Neo-druidism
Neopaganism
New Buddhist movements
New Humanism
Non-Rabbinic sects
Nootka mythology
Norse mythology

Northern indigenous religions
Occultism
Oceanic religions
Old Catholicism
Oneness Pentecostalism
Oomoto
Oriental Orthodoxy
Orthodox Judaism
Pawnee mythology
Pentecostalism
People's Temple
Persian religions
Pharisees/Pharisaism
Polynesian mythology
Presbyterianism
Process Church of the Final
    Judgment
Protestantism
Puritans
Pygmy mythology
Rabbinic Judaism
Raelism
Rastafari
Reformed churches
Reform Judaism
Religious Society of Friends
Restorationism
Right-Hand Path religions
Roman Catholicism
Roman religion
Rosicrucian
Russian Orthodox Church
Sadducees
Salish mythology
Sai Baba movement
Samaritanism
Santería
Science Grounded Religion
Scientology
Seax-Wica
Secular Humanism
Seneca mythology
Seventh-day Adventists
Shafi'i
Shaivism
Shaktism
Shi'a Islam (Shi'ite)
Shinto

Sikhism
Sithism
Slavic mythology
Smartism
Spiritism
Spiritual Humanism
Spiritualism
Spirituality
Sufism (a form of Islamic
    mysticism)
Summum
Sunni Islam
Syriac Christianity
Taoism
Temple of Set
Tenrikyo
THC Ministry
Thelema
Theosophy
Theravada
Tibetan Buddhism
Tsimshian mythology
Tumbuka mythology
Tuvaluan mythology
Twelvers
Umbanda
Unification Church (Moonies)
Unitarian Universalism
Unitarianism
Universal Life Church
Ute mythology
Vaishnavism
Vajrayana
Vedanta
Voudun (Voodoo)
Wahhabi
Wicca
Winnebago mythology
Winti
Yezidis
Yoism
Yoruba mythology
Yukaghir mythology
Zen
Zoroastrianism
Zulu mythology
Zuni mythology
Zurvanism

Whoa! This is a pretty extensive list indeed. I sincerely apologize if any group was left out. It was unintentional. With all this diversity in belief systems, we're left with the big question "Who is right?" If all the Christians indeed are following the one true way, is the other 66 percent of the population really destined for eternal damnation? What if the Muslims are the ones to be rewarded for their beliefs? That would mean that fully 80 percent of the world has gotten it wrong and will be infidels. When I take all of this into account, it seems to be a very inefficient cycle of creation and destruction by God. At that rate, the human race would be reaching extinction. Yet the human population continues to grow. Bottom line is that the fundamental goal is the same—live an honorable, fulfilling life and be subsequently rewarded by your respective afterlife.

Initially, I had real trouble believing the world actually works that way. I joked to myself that if this were really the scenario, why didn't the various gods fight it out rather than allow all these human wars? Imagine what a show it would be if these various religious entities were to duke it out in heaven. Perhaps a football-friendly, single-elimination tournament (aka the Heavenly Cup) would be the answer. The first round would pit the Jesus Saints against the Shiva Destroyers. The other bracket would include the Muhammad Warriors versus the Buddhist Strikers. The winners could move on to the next bracket and so on, until one reigned supreme and victorious. The grand prize would be complete devotion from all of humanity.

Yes, this made for a fanciful daydream for the end of human wars. My practical self was just as confused as ever by all the religious diversity. None of it seemed to make any sense to me.

I realized the best approach could be to simplify—just refer to all this diversity of faith as God. You may prefer Yahweh, Allah, Lord, Father, Almighty, Bhagwan, Ishwar, Devata, Buddha, or Jehovah instead. Regardless, you either believe in God or you don't. Those who don't believe in God call themselves atheists. In some ways I can understand their frustrations, given some of the violence and levels of extremism in our world. Their skepticism is rooted in a lack of proof. Is there absolute, 100 percent proof that God *does* exist? Many religions make this claim, but in reality, I don't think so. Well then, is there absolute, 100 percent proof that God *doesn't* exist? Once again, I don't think so.

Given this dilemma, I'll take my chances that God really does exist. Why? Simply put, the stakes are too high. Why miss out on one of the greatest possibilities mankind has ever known? If indeed there is some type of eternal life or salvation, I wouldn't want to miss out on the party. If I am dead wrong, guess what? I will never know about it. I will be decomposing six feet under without a worry in the world.

The ways people believe in God are extremely variable, as you have seen from the earlier list. Hence the common use of the word "faith," which can be used interchangeably with hope, belief, or trust in worship of single or multiple deities, or perhaps in spiritual teachings or doctrine. Most commonly, the word faith is used in the context of people having faith in God's existence.

Spirituality persists in every known culture. What is its real meaning and function? Maybe we pursue what connects us, whether a god or more deeply something within ourselves, in a search for what makes us human. Medical science can't find a gene or neuron that fully explains us. What is love, anger, or passion? I am sure that if anyone discovered the biochemical composition of love, there'd be a booming market for its replicated love potion.

There is no such thing. Or it has yet to be discovered. We have many theories about our very human emotions and sensibilities, but no explanations. I wish it was plainly black and white, but for now it's a gray zone. My theory is as up for debate as any other, but perhaps it is the search for an understanding of the gray zone— this undefined link between the physical and what mystifies us— that inspires spirituality.

Thinking about this prompted me to read about many religions and helped awaken my spiritual renewal. I began to find it worthwhile to turn my attentions not only to the disagreements and wars sparked by religion, but once again to the potential for good it brings as well.

The singular question everyone can ask is, "Does God actually exist?" As I mentioned before, there is no 100 percent answer either way, no matter what claims may be out there. However, just because we can't sense something doesn't mean it doesn't exist. How do we hear or sense God? What if we had a God frequency? Our antennae could be our spiritual minds. Perhaps the only way to tune in to this frequency would be through meditation, prayer, and so on. Of course this is just a theory, albeit an intriguing one. It may be completely off base for some and perhaps logical for others. I am sure there are many more conceptual ideas out there.

Regardless, I fully respect all the varying opinions on spiritual matters. None of us know all the answers. We all may return to dust at the end of our lives, and that's all she wrote. Still I hope you will ask yourself, whether or not you find literal truth in religion or faith, what's the real negative of utilizing spirituality as a source of hope, comfort, and coping? I invite believers and nonbelievers alike to consider this: What would it mean to get your best ROI on spiritual life?

GETTING THE MOST
FROM SPIRITUALITY

After all of my searching and wondering whether there really is one single, correct way to be religious or spiritual, I began to notice something. No matter what the specifics, there are certain core benefits to holding beliefs and practices of this nature. Despite the small and sometimes huge differences between paths, the common threads seem to be doing a whole lot of good. In fact, there is so much universal seeking of these paths and ways of understanding the world that spirituality emerges easily as one of our Core Assets.

What does spirituality bring to the table in terms of ROI? Spirituality gives people a sense of hope. When there is stress and adversity in life, a simple prayer or a time to sit and send out a positive intention can soothe raw emotions. Spirituality also provides a sense of calm and inner peace. Meditation on God, a saint or avatar, or a particular wonder of nature, or simply calling up the belief in a benevolent and ordered universe, has the power to iron out the frayed edges of daily life.

Religion is particularly good at providing you with a sense of purpose and direction. When a person believes with all his or her heart that he or she has a divine assignment to follow in the footsteps of Jesus, to make a pilgrimage to the Ganges River, or to uphold the Buddhist precepts, life automatically has focus. Life will always be full of surprises, but the spiritual path gives a person some answers about what is at the top of the to-do list and how to proceed when the going gets tough.

Comfort is another wonderful benefit of the Core Asset of spirituality. For some people, the idea that we humans are just tiny specks stuck on one planet out of billions that arose completely by chance in the aftermath of the Big Bang is just too much to bear. These same people may feel much more balanced by believing or sensing that there is more to the story, that somewhere there is a plan and a reason for our lives. If your belief system includes elements like a god intent on an essence of universal love that pervades everything in the world, it can be a source of great comfort.

Spirituality also provides a very good coping mechanism. I'm sure many of us know someone who got into some kind of trouble, and the crisis triggered a quick spiritual awakening. In my own life, I can remember a time when my family and I were on a flight leaving Dallas, Texas. After a while in the air, we hit a serious lightning storm. The turbulence was intense. The plane dropped altitude very suddenly a couple of times, and a little fear monster in the back of my mind had me wondering if we'd make it out alive. Even through my skepticism, I found myself reciting prayers. It was as if my spirituality instinct just kicked in.

Obviously we made it home and lived to tell the tale. The skeptic in me still wondered if saying prayers could have had any actual effect on the outcome. Ultimately I decided it mattered little; what it did give me for sure was a focus to find strength when I needed it most. If some supernatural assistance interceded on our behalf as well, then I am extra grateful.

My family and I were very fortunate that day. Tragedy, death, and general bad situations are a fact of the human condition. When these things happen, spirituality often comes to the rescue.

The rituals associated with spirituality can also provide very good ROI. The encouraging thing is that it doesn't seem as though a great battle of the land, sea, and sky gods is necessary after all. The same benefits seem to apply no matter what religious foundation you choose or rituals you practice.

Every religion has ways of reaching out to God or diving deep into the inner self. Ritual practices involving prayers, chanting, dancing, and singing are common elements of these expressions. The languages and cultures may be different. The chants may be Gregorian or Vedic. A Santeria prayer to the ancestors might seem entirely different from a Catholic petition to a patron saint. Your culture's everyday ritual might be another's bizarre spectacle, and vice versa. However, one common thread that runs through the variation is connection. These practices help individuals and communities feel a connection to God, to others who worship in similar ways, and to those for whom they seek to help or heal by way of offering these practices. Feeling connected is a deep-seated human desire, and spiritual practices such as these provide a great avenue for it.

As a medical doctor, I was taught to consider evidence-based medicine from strong clinical research backed by legitimate, randomized, double-blind trials when applicable. This has its merits when considering various treatments with medications. However, even this has its limitations in some respects when it comes to quantifying the surgical or psychological effectiveness of treatments. Observational and anecdotal evidence eventually has to come into play.

With this in mind, there are studies that show measurable improvement of physical and mental health among those who practice religious or spiritual rituals. For example, reciting the rosary and chanting yoga mantras can help regulate cardiovascular rhythms. Prayer and attendance at church services can help alleviate stress, which is implicated as the catalyst of many ailments of body and mind. Regular religious service attendance has been associated with a lower risk of depression as well.

Anecdotal evidence has long suggested that meditation brings about a sense of well-being for those who practice it. Some evidence shows it may actually synchronize diffuse neural networks in the brain, with lasting effects well beyond the period of the actual meditation, eventually making changes that seem to be permanent and positive. Even in the face of difficult circumstances such as confronting cancer, prayer can help. A prayer practice can kick in the biochemical mechanism that assists our strength and will. It may not have the magic bullet to cure the disease, but it can go a long way toward getting someone through mental and physical hardships.

Psychiatrist Carl Jung believed that to perceive spiritual and religious experience is part of the fabric of being human, and to ignore that part of ourselves is as egregious as ignoring physical health. He would likely not be surprised by the many links between the two we seem to be uncovering today.

There is one more benefit to spirituality that we shouldn't let go by without a mention. Unlike a consultation with virtually any professional, a conversation with God is absolutely free! There is no insurance premium or co-pay. There is no waiting list, and there is never a need to take a rain check. God is always in the office. If you are so inclined, it can't hurt to go to straight to the top with all your joys as well as all that ails you.

Religious rituals are no replacement for sound medical advice and procedures when they are necessary. However, it is exciting that empirical evidence is coming in to suggest some of these practices that have developed over centuries can give a bona fide boost to health. There's nothing wrong with having extra tools in the toolbox to improve wellness—especially when they may also help us find meaning along the way.

Now let's review the main opportunities for a positive ROI on spirituality. Spirituality can give us:

- Hope

- Inner peace and calm

- Comfort

- A way to cope with adversity

- A sense of connection

- Physical and mental health benefits

- A free consultation!

However, we've already alluded to the other side of the coin. How does the law of diminishing returns function in the realm of the spiritual?

WHEN RELIGION GOES WRONG

I can understand the frustration and criticism of the cynics who see the downside of religion. The law of diminishing returns works just the same even in this part of life that can bring forth the highs of ecstatic praise, the feeling of inherent connection with all living beings, and the inspiration for remarkable altruism. As with all of our Core Assets, you can draw a graph of its effects. At the top of the curve is the sweet spot where spirituality does its highest good for individuals and humanity. Religion played a major role in fueling the leadership and activism of Gandhi and the great humanitarian works of Mother Teresa. As the curve turns downward and then plunges to its low point, it depicts spirituality increasingly out of balance. It is hard for most of us even to imagine the extreme distortion of religion that continues to propel hateful protests of the intolerant. Unfortunately, when religion goes wrong, it can go very, very wrong.

The concept of the one right way is a downside of religion and spirituality. Some religions teach that their way is the only way. Adhering to that belief is fine if it fortifies your worldview and remains a positive esteem builder, but it can become problematic if it is a source of conflict with others. If you come to believe that all people of different faiths are evil or ignorant whose souls are to be condemned in the afterlife, how positive could your interactions be on this planet?

Another way spirituality can cause trouble in a person's life is by becoming the only thing that matters. When a particular spiritual system or spiritual musing in general becomes the only concern, finances, friendships, and even basic health care can suffer. No matter how strong the belief, giving up all worldly possessions to a religious organization or a charismatic individual without serious consideration and forethought may lead to little more than personal ruin and disillusionment. As with all the Core Assets, the benefits of spirituality are felt most fully when balanced with all other important aspects of life.

Rules that are too rigid or become their own endpoints, as opposed to the means to spiritual discovery, can pose problems. A person may at first appreciate a religious path for a sense of kinship with others. In time he may find that the rules—and the beliefs around punishment for breaking those rules—are so stringent that life has tipped from camaraderie and hope to anxiety and fear. If you discover that your religion blocks you from exploring free thought, or you find yourself paralyzed with shame over deviations from religious law, it may be wise to consider a path more in keeping with your nature.

A spirituality that works well for an individual is one that helps him or her find a positive place in the universe. The paths we follow often help us answer the age-old question, "In the grand scheme of things, where do I fit in?" Sadly, some individuals or whole groups may find themselves devalued within the belief system of their origin or choice. If, for example, a woman's place is far below a man's, according to a given religion, a woman in that religion might suffer emotional distress or even mistreatment from other believers. Her ROI would be diminished because the positive input she gets back from her religion is quite likely a good deal less than she gives of herself on its behalf. A higher rate of neuroses has been observed among groups that are sidelined by their own religion.

Many religious beliefs offer guidelines for how best to deal with matters of the body. Sometimes, however, religious organizations feature very specific mandates that may have negative effects on physical health. According to one interpretation of the Bible, taking a blood transfusion is against scripture. Yet refusal of a transfusion at a critical time could cost a life. Various groups may refuse all vaccinations and medical treatments. To a group that does not recognize depression as an authentic mental health issue, prayer, not therapy or medication, may be the only accepted treatment. Undue psychological distress could result for someone suffering from real emotional tribulations or chemical imbalance. A denomination that asks believers to handle poisonous snakes poses a direct and immediate health threat. Even dietary practices based on spiritual belief systems could bring about challenges, for example, for a diabetic who would do well to eat at regular intervals rather than fasting.

It is up to individuals to make the ultimate decisions on how much to adhere to literal doctrine when it comes to health matters. Some may be willing to take on higher risks in order to avoid certain procedures. But to keep the ROI on physical health in balance with the spiritual, it is definitely worthwhile to reconsider any doctrine that stands in strong opposition to medical advice.

Some of the saddest examples of the distortion of religion can be found in the world news nearly any day of the week. You only need to turn on the TV or go online for a short time to hear a tragic story of a suicide bomber, a kidnapping, a shooting spree, or a continuing, full-on war. It is terrible to realize just how much of the violence is based on religion. Strong convictions are one thing; extremism is quite another. Extremism often breeds isolation from anyone who may offer varied ideas. Separation breeds mistrust, and intense mistrust can descend into outright hatred.

If we've outlined the benefits of spirituality to include peace, comfort, and connection, it seems that extremism is religion twisted to become its polar opposite. Other than through some profoundly misguided sense of belonging, extremism filtered through any religious guise offers none of the positive ROI that spirituality can offer and thrusts division and destruction in its place. Of course you should understand that extremism is generally a very small part of any religion. What the media outlets tend to show are the outliers that help generate ratings. The normal, less-extreme practices that are more prevalent in various societies simply would be too boring to capture the interest of the viewing public.

Here are some of the problems that can take over when spiritual concerns are taken too far:

- Conflict sparked by the idea of "one right way"
- Consequences from loss of interest in all else
- Emotional distress brought on by overly rigid rules
- Low self-esteem or devaluation of individuals by the belief system
- Health risks from religious laws that are contrary to medical advice
- Isolation and violence as products of extremism

CAPS FOR ROI ON SPIRITUALITY

These **C**ORE **A**SSET **P**ROTECTION **S**TRATEGIES can help you hold on to the best that spirituality has to offer without falling into the negative zone.

1. **Practice religious tolerance for a balanced life and higher ROI.** Religious intolerance is not only destructive to the balance of your Core Assets; it is also destructive to society. Let's face it—diverse belief systems and religions are here to stay. Although a few may dominate any given region or country, the likelihood of a religious monoculture is less and less likely. As the population and worldwide communication continue to grow, so does religious diversity. Can you imagine the collective ROI if society diverted its energy toward peace? This may be a very idealistic point of view, but each of our efforts can and does make a difference.

   Choosing tolerance enhances your well-being and that of the culture all around you. Don't waste your valuable currencies of time and energy worrying about others and their different beliefs. There is a significant opportunity-cost impact from doing so. Instead, consider expending your currencies elsewhere. Your education, love life, sports activities, or leisure is waiting for you. Remember, your time is limited. Use it wisely.

2. **Embrace the diversity.** It is comforting to find commonalities among people with beliefs and practices similar to your own. However, you can take religious tolerance a step further by actively embracing the differences. Accepting the differences of others is important. As humans, diversifying just seems to be part of our nature, even within a single religious

system. Christianity breaks down into Orthodox, Catholic, and Protestant. Protestants break down into Lutherans, Baptists, Methodists, Presbyterians, and Anglicans. In Judaism you have Orthodox, Conservative, and Reform. Muslims include Sunnis, Shias, Wahhabis, and Sufis. In the Hindu world, Vishnu, Shiva, and Devi are worshipped in many forms. Rather than looking at the diversity with suspicion, curious acceptance is a better way to go.

Sometimes differences in our religions make us feel good about our own affinities. Imagine if everyone wore the same Versace outfit. It wouldn't feel special at all. If you are one of only a few wearing it, it feels special. That doesn't mean you need to chastise the other person for what they're wearing. Likewise, if you feel especially good about your religion, there's nothing at all wrong with that. Enjoy it, and enjoy the colorful display put on by everyone around you, too.

3. **Don't be afraid to critique your own faith.** Following a faith does not mean checking your brain at the door. Pay attention to the ideas being taught. How do they resonate for you? If you're a champion for peace, you should consider walking away from those messengers and interpreters who preach its opposite. Misguided leaders prey on the insecurities and vulnerabilities of their constituencies. You have the power to move away from their teachings. Without an audience, there is no platform for them to grow their power and influence.

If at its core your religion really does teach peace, you will not be abandoning your religion but only the ignorance that has been taught in its name. There are hundreds of other congregations, synagogues, mosques, and temples to choose from that deliver positive messages of peace, tolerance, and well-being. You would do well to gravitate toward one of those. Alternatively, you can simply be a good citizen and a conscientious person by discovering a positive spirituality of your own volition.

4. **Be careful how you interpret your religion or spiritual path.** Most religions provide guidance through metaphors that are not meant to be taken literally. Such misinterpretations are often responsible for grave misunderstandings and subsequent intolerance. Religion in its purest form is unadulterated by an intermediary or third party. Therefore there is no substitute for reading your spiritual texts on your own, without the influence of others.

    Due to constraints of time and, in many cases, a language barrier, it certainly is okay to outsource religious teachings to a spiritual leader. Just as you would when seeking out any other professional, remember to choose your leader wisely.

5. **Let religion fit your personal comfort level.** Some Christians may have problems going to church every weekend. Some Jewish men may find it uncomfortable to wear a kippah. Some Muslim women may prefer not to cover their heads with a hijab. The list goes on and on. Do differences like these make the individuals less devoted to their chosen faiths? Not necessarily. Exercise your freedom to practice what works for you and leave the rest.

    On the other hand, some of you may find the social cost of forging new ground is too great. In that case you may have a better ROI by conforming in order to avoid conflict with members of your community. Weigh the relative returns of each possible action, and you will know how best to proceed.

6. **Don't hesitate to give yourself a religious or spiritual time-out if you find yourself overly conflicted.** Spiritual distress may arise if you feel a sense of anger, disillusionment, or fear. The emotions may be projected toward God or toward others around you. Recognize the tendency to want to externalize and avoid these frustrations and misgivings. Instead you may wish to harness them by redirecting your spiritual energy toward things such as additional prayers or rituals.

Or you may want to stop engaging spiritual issues directly for some time. Allow yourself to take a break. Not only will you continue to grow spiritually during your time away, but you will also avoid undue stress and regretful actions. A spiritual time-out is a great opportunity to be alert to how your other Core Assets are affected by your spirituality. Have they been compromised by too much religion? Are other parts of your life suffering because you've been avoiding seeking spirituality in the way it calls to you most strongly? Do you notice you miss your regular practices? Your answers will help you maintain balance. Your spirituality, balanced in just the right way, will fit your other Core Assets. You will enjoy its great benefits as you move toward realizing your maximum ROI.

9

Make Time Matter: Your ROI on Life

We've gone over a lot in the past seven chapters. We've looked at subjects from how to create a balanced spiritual life to suggestions for beginning an exercise program. We've covered the benefits to society of an educated population as well as the importance of eye contact and confidence when establishing a new relationship. We've discussed discretionary spending and smoking cessation. All of that is a lot to think about, and you might well feel a bit overwhelmed with information.

That was intentional. It was meant to be a starting point for you as you gather information to make the right choices in your life. Did you forget about Integrative Decision Making already? Remember steps 3 and 4, developing and analyzing your options. So far we gathered as much relevant information as we could so you can start making informed decisions. I just wanted to double-check.

Like I mentioned before, life doesn't show up with one small, easily solved concern followed by the next thing that needs your attention cruising toward you at a peaceful, easy pace. No, life is full of complex situations and unexpected circumstances. Nearly all of us at some time have felt that life throws so much at us at once; it would be easier just to duck and hide away from it all. Bringing together so many issues in this book was designed to create awareness of just how much in our lives needs attention, and how imperative it is that we do our best to seek balance.

By taking a single-focus approach, it would be all too easy to beat a well-worn path to disappointment. This book has brought the picture together and gotten you thinking about not a single, but *all* of your Core Assets. My hope is you'll keep your eyes open to the complexity of real-life situations and give your attention to doing what it takes to grow and improve at each new opportunity. I hope you will take this book as an invitation to consider your priorities deeply and use it as a guide to achieving your personal best.

What is our biggest challenge to mastering all that life throws our way? It is remembering that our resources are limited. We have five basic currencies we invest to gain our Core Assets: labor or sweat equity, emotions, social interactions, and money represent a big portion of what we exchange for obtaining jobs, relationships, good health, and all the things we strive to achieve. However, time is by far the most important of the five. U.S. congressman John Randolph (1773–1833) said, "Time is at once the most valuable and the most perishable of all our possessions." The truth of this statement remains just as pertinent today. Let it stand as a reminder to us all to make our decisions wisely.

We can easily choose the level of sweat equity to put into a project or, with effort, learn how to manage our emotions. The amount of money any one of us has will change over time, and though it is a great tool in society, it is not the ultimate measure of happiness. One thing is true for all of us: we have only so much time. Unfortunately, of all the currencies, time is generally taken the most for granted. It is easily squandered and often valued the least. When we are younger, we tend to think we have all the time in the world. When we get older, we look back wistfully, wishing to have back the time that has passed.

This is why time management is so important. Only by being truly aware of how fleeting time is in our lives can we understand that the time we do have is absolutely priceless. It is our most valuable currency and our most limited resource. It can't be bought no matter how rich you are or how many material goods you acquire. Nor can it be recovered; once lost, it is gone forever.

Your time is yours. As you recognize this and take control of your time, you will become a truly powerful player in your own destiny. So let's assimilate all we've talked about and focus on how to harness and allocate time. Once it's managed, you can optimize your Core Assets for maximum ROI with time on your side.

TIME MANAGEMENT—THE BASICS

Time management is simply being prepared, organized, and planning ahead. Many people who prefer a "take it as it comes" attitude hold the idea that organizing and planning will lead to a regimented life with no room for spontaneity. This is a common misconception, and nearly the opposite is true. By being more prepared, you will find yourself more at ease, with more time and flexibility for spontaneous fun.

If you are one of the many people who have long believed you can't control time, allow yourself to reconsider. Put your fears, tendency to procrastinate, and concerns about not knowing where to start aside. Today is the day to begin changing that attitude for the better. By managing your time, you can work smarter, not harder.

Think about it this way: if you are able to save just one hour a day, that works out to twenty-three extra days of waking hours available to you each year. Saving two hours a day is the equivalent of taking back forty-six days per year that would otherwise be lost. These examples alone show just how much time you can recover with a simple shift in thinking and by taking action. What a gift it would be to have all those days back to do more and to achieve your goals in life.

The first big step is to discover or admit where and how you're wasting time. Do you start out briefly checking for important email and wind up spending hours responding to frivolous messages in your inbox? Do you veg out a little too long in front of the TV at night? How about your phone calls? Are you yakking it up beyond basic business and the important staying-in-touch moments? And while the Internet is a profound development and has ushered in endless opportunity, it has also brought us the opportunity for 24/7 entertainment and distraction.

You may already know your particular poison. Is it a social networking site, instant messaging with your friend during your most productive hours, or reality television? Maybe you're a news junkie or get lost on your favorite celebrities' blogs. Whether you're into horror flicks, sports, music trivia, or super-cute cat videos, it is important to know when enough is enough.

Here are five big actions you can take toward managing your time effectively.

PRIORITIZE

Decide which activities are important and which are not so important. Making lists can help you. Begin your day with the most important tasks so you don't chase details while forgetting the big picture. Stay focused, learn efficiency, and streamline your activities while you are doing your important work. You need recreation, too, so enjoy the appropriate amount of time you've set aside for relaxation.

STAY ORGANIZED

This is a tough one for a lot of people, but finding techniques to keep things in order is absolutely worth the effort. Otherwise the constant need to search for a document, a pen, the shirt you plan to wear to the interview, or the email you saw in your inbox earlier in the day is a huge time waster.

STAY HEALTHY

Believe it or not, your health regimen can have a positive effect. By getting plenty of sleep, exercising regularly, and eating a good diet, you will improve your focus and concentration. A good health routine in turn improves overall efficiency in getting your work done in less time.

DELEGATE

Many of us have had it drummed into our heads that it's always better to do something yourself than to hire someone else. This is not always so. The last time I decided to take on a home painting project, it took me an entire day. The next time I had a similar project, I broke down and hired someone—and that person got the job done in about two hours.

When is it best for you to delegate? A good way to find out is to calculate your personal hourly rate: take your annual salary, divide it by two, and drop three zeros at the end. If you work independently, average your typical fee and calculate what you make per hour. Then look at the task you have at hand. Could you pay a painter less than your hourly rate? When I did that first paint job myself, it was costly because I could have paid a painter much less than the income I could have generated in the time it took me to do it. It was also a huge opportunity cost because I could have been spending that time on maximizing another ROI.

You may want to delegate more than household tasks. What about hiring an assistant or an administrator to take care of everyday tasks that take up your time? Evaluate each task to see whether delegating (outsourcing) or DIY (insourcing) will provide the highest ROI.

ACT NOW

Procrastination is a big time waster. By putting off a task rather than completing it in the moment, you usually have to spend time reacclimating yourself to the task or rushing to catch up to get it done on time. By not finishing things that were already started, you easily create a pileup of future time-consuming activities. When you are confronted with something on your to-do list you know needs attention at the time, make "do it now" your motto.

PUT IT ALL TOGETHER

As you can see, time management isn't just about keeping a calendar. It's about maintaining focus, getting things done in an orderly way, and being savvy enough to know when you're not the one for the job. The next big piece of the puzzle is something we discussed early on in this book: Integrative Decision Making.

Essentially, every choice you make throughout the day affects how you use your time. The better the decisions you make for yourself, the more time you will save for better uses. Let's take a few moments to note some silly decisions that lower the ROI on your hard-earned assets and waste precious time:

- **Bad behavior and poor choices** make big headlines for plenty of celebrities, sports figures, artists, and politicians. However, the poor choices that may be good for tabloid media do little good in the lives of the rich and famous or the rest of us. Getting into trouble with bad behavior leads to problems like suspensions, job loss, and legal issues, and it can wind up costing a lot of money. To top it off, the time lost can be staggering. It might have taken you years to build a career and a great reputation only to have to try to rebuild it after it all comes crashing down.

- **Poor spending habits and bad investments** affect more than just your wallet. Losing money wastes time. Not only is it painful to lose the money, but also all the time spent earning it is squandered.

- **Losing a relationship** may be painful and complex because it often combines stress and emotional pain along with the loss of the connection. Divorce is a triple whammy because loss of money due to lawyers and settlements is par for the course. With any ending of a relationship, you can never reclaim all the time you poured into trying to make it work.

- **Unsafe practices** were touched on in the last chapter. An injury that results from poor driving habits could exact a cost in injury or disability. Not only does that translate into lost wages and a lower quality of life, but also think of the countless hours you could spend in recuperation and rehabilitation.

- **Bad day-to-day dietary choices** make a difference. If you eat a medium-sized donut, you will consume 100 to 150 calories. To burn those empty calories, you'll need to spend twenty-five minutes walking at a pace of three miles per hour. If you kick it up a notch and jog at five miles per hour, you'll still spend ten to fifteen minutes counteracting that donut. So a quick, two-minute chow down has effectively taken up to twenty-five minutes of your time.

On the positive side, time spent upfront on staying healthy and on prevention of disease will save not only money but also countless hours on treating diseases after they develop. Learning proper exercise techniques saves you time you would otherwise spend on injury and recovery.

While I maintain that spirituality is one of our Core Assets, I have heard flack from some people who say spirituality and religion are complete wastes of time. I disagree—these practices and beliefs are healthy and positive when they nurture, inspire, and serve as a source of strength while being integrated into the rest of your life. However, when moderation morphs into extremism, religion takes over crucial time that should be spent on the other Core Assets.

That leads to the most important point about Integrative Decision Making. Ultimately you have the knowledge, the inner wisdom, and the power to control the major aspects of your life in order to reap the greatest joys. It all comes down to how you choose to spend your time, in conjunction with the other basic life currencies, to achieve your maximum ROI. We've looked at enough cautionary tales about how things can go awry. You have what it takes to use your Integrative Decision Making to get the balance right.

When you look at the big picture, which of the Core Assets you have discovered are most important to you? As you've processed the material in this book, have you discovered your relationships and family life take precedence over your career? Do you favor the development of your intellect and spirit more than the pursuit of cash? Maybe you are most excited about focusing on physical health and believe all other good things flow from feeling good inside and out.

The best part about contemplating these questions is that you don't have to choose among Core Assets while forgetting the rest. We all get to savor the good times and take on the challenges in each of these areas. Most of us gravitate naturally toward one or a few of the Core Assets that are of primary importance to us. The others still carry weight but may seem less prominent. Allow yourself to take an honest assessment of your priorities, recognize where to concentrate your focus, and keep this information in mind as you make your life decisions. The integration of Core Assets that emerges is likely to be the personal blend that is right to use becomes a joy when you are applying them to goals you've determined really matter.

The amount of information discussed in this book about dealing with our Core Assets is not only to illustrate the way life hurls choices our way at high velocity. It is also meant to remind you that with each decision comes a new chance for self-improvement. Every new person, every new idea, and each new opportunity presents us with a chance to grow. What was your response in a similar situation in the past? What would you like to do this time to make your life better, more meaningful, closer in alignment with all the Core Assets have to offer?

To make those leaps in growth, you have to make the conscious choice to improve. Take a good look at your wants and needs, accept your strengths and weaknesses, and commit to enacting the changes that will make your life its very best.

Moving toward a happy, balanced life of self-fulfillment takes vision, planning, and our scarcest resource: time. It also takes patience and reinforcement. The friends you'll want to keep around are the ones who encourage you to shine.

Like all fallible human beings, you probably won't be able to accomplish all your goals at once. You may choose to work on only a few things at first to build a foundation. I hope you will allow this book to continue to be a resource. You may want to read it several times. Use it as a reference, for reinforcement, and as a source of information. Designing your most fulfilling life is not something you can undertake overnight.

Of course there will be times when you may fail or relapse into an old behavior that no longer serves you well. That's okay. Regroup, recommit, and stay on course. If you put your mind to it, you can do it. As you move forward, a great ROI for me would be to hear about improvements you've made in your life. Shoot me an email or send me an old-school letter to let me know how you're doing.

Remember: Our course in life does not follow a straight path. There will be ups and downs. Think of it as a stock chart. You will want to avoid extreme volatility, during which you climb to the highest of highs only to crash and burn to the lowest of lows. By making a commitment to maximize your ROI on life, that path will continue its upward trend, and you will certainly reach your summit of optimal living.

Acknowledgments

I have so many people to thank for their support throughout the process of writing this book that it's difficult to know where to begin. To keep this short and sweet, I would like to thank all of you who have influenced me throughout my journey in life. Without your inspiration and encouragement this book never would have happened. You know who you are, so please give yourself a pat on the back.

More specifically, I want to acknowledge my wife, Priti, who has been a steady boat of reason and stability. I also want to acknowledge my two young sons, Milan and Arjun, both of whom are still too young to understand what Daddy has written. Your zest and energy fill me with joy and hope for the future.

About the Author

Sanjay Jain is a US-trained, board certified physician with more than fifteen years of clinical experience. He holds certifications in Diagnostic Radiology, Integrative Medicine, and Healthcare Quality and Management. He has diversified experience in private practice, academic, and integrated multispecialty settings. He is a former assistant professor at The Ohio State University Medical School, where he also obtained his MBA at The Fisher School of Business.

Sanjay has served on numerous committees at nearly every level of his professional career. He is a member of the American Roentgen Ray Society, American College of Sports Medicine, American College of Forensic Medicine, American Association of Integrative Medicine, and American Institute for Healthcare Quality. He has delivered talks both domestically and internationally.

Keep in touch with Sanjay via Twitter @sanjayjainmd.

Also don't forget to visit him on Facebook, Google+, and his website sanjayjainmd.com.